ENTREPRENEUR IN A SMALL COUNTRY

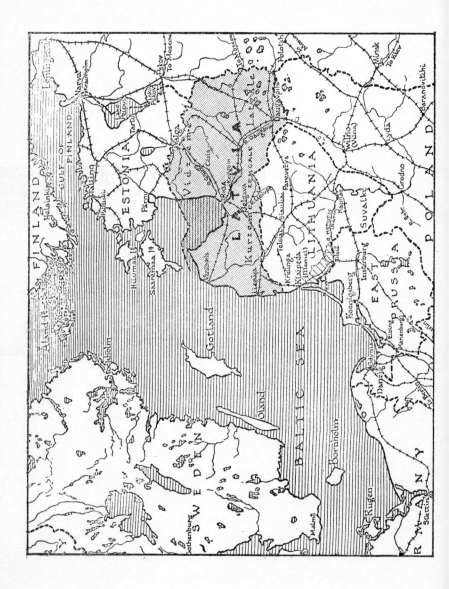

ENTREPRENEUR
IN A SMALL COUNTRY

*A Case Study Against the Background
of the Latvian Economy, 1919-1940*

Nicholas Balabkins and
Arnolds Aizsilnieks

An Exposition-University Book

Exposition Press   Hicksville, New York

FIRST EDITION

Library of Congress Catalog Card Number: 74-21436

ISBN 0-682-48158-0

Printed in the United States of America

To the memory of
ROBERTS HIRSS, 1895-1972

Contents

Contents

Acknowledgments

Numerous individuals contributed to the writing of this volume. Mrs. Alma Hirss, the widow of Roberts Hirss, was a valued source of guidance and support for both of us. My colleagues at Lehigh University, Oles M. Smolansky, Joseph B. McFadden and Jere Knight, read all or parts of the draft and made numerous suggestions and improvements. Dr. Gerhard Teich of the *Library of the Institut für Weltwirtschaft* suggested a number of useful references. To all of them we should like to express our thanks.

A. A. and N. B.

Preface

Collaboration always has its advantages and its drawbacks. Initially it signals a meeting of minds and a desire to further a common goal. At the same time it is difficult for one of the partners not to defer to the other and still retain his identity. In this case both authors were born in the same country, from which they are both political exiles. One has dedicated a number of years of his scholarly career to a study of his native land; the other views his native country chiefly as part of his ongoing interest in the economic problems of small countries. Both of us share the hope that this volume may prove to have wider interest than its rather narrow historical focus. Thus, where we speak with a common voice we shall use the editorial "we" and subsequently identify the individual voice where it seems necessary to do so.

In the wake of World War II, a large number of small but sovereign countries came into being. Today, in contrast to the older industrialized countries, they are generally referred to as the developing or less-developed countries. These recently-sovereign nations are having great difficulty to make ends meet on their own. In fact, many of them suffer from abject poverty and even starvation. For years, the rich, industrialized countries have been supporting these new, poor states by sending them millions of dollars worth of equipment and food. Yet these millions have evaporated like raindrops in the vast wastes of a desert. The idea is widely held that lack of physical capital is primarily responsible for the underdevelopment and stagnation. It is, however, our belief that the greatest obstacle to structural change is the lack of private initiative and entrepreneurship. When private initiative can flourish, it usually finds ways and means to obtain the necessary capital funds. Conversely, ample investment funds, per se, will not generate structural change and development if private initiative is lacking. During the centuries of feudal rule that prevailed in the society of what are now the developing countries, private initiative and entrepreneurship had virtually no place. As a result, entrepreneurship is still in its infancy there today. Furthermore, in most developing countries, the institutional social structures, with their archaic laws and customs, have had a negative effect on the modernization efforts. For example, tribalism and the "expanded" family concept is one such institution. In these societies, it is an unwritten law that all members of a particular tribe, or of a particular family, have the right to stay with the wealthiest member of the tribe or family and to demand food and shelter. This ancient level of egalitarianism is one of the factors which has, we speculate, effected negatively the supply of indigenous entrepreneurs in the developing countries.

To foster structural change in this type of institutional setting, the governments of the developing countries have taken the economic reins in their own hands. They form "national" enterprises and set up state monopolies in rapid succession in order to shape the economic life of their countries in accordance with their own ideas and wishes. However, such a "dirigiste" or "statist" economic system stymies the growth of free initiative and private entrepreneurship because no government can compete with the private sector. Similarly, as in a feudal society where everybody expected everything from the feudal lord or his court, in today's "statist" countries everybody expects everything from the governments and their bureaucracies.

Despite the great role entrepreneurship has played in the economic life of the industrialized countries, it has not been sufficiently studied. Nor has it been adequately dealt with in contemporary economic theory. Not all economists consider entrepreneurship to be an independent factor of production. But whatever the reason, the entrepreneurship factor is simply ignored by those economists who remain captive of the idea that there are only three primary factors of production: labor, capital, and land.

In the face of all the above considerations, we have attempted in this volume to demonstrate concretely and realistically what role entrepreneurship can play in the evolutionary process of a new and small country. Latvia's economic experience during its period of independence, 1918-1940, that is, prior to its lawless occupation by the Soviet Union, offered an illuminating example. In addition, there was available the unique material on the large, privately-owned textile firm, *Rīgas Audums,* that flourished in Latvia during the 1920s and 1930s due to the entrepreneurial genius of one man. An examination of its activities demonstrated to us that sprawling bureaucratic controls of economic life, under conditions of nominal private ownership of the means of production, do not offer the most expeditious climate for fostering economic growth and the material well-being of a people. Quite the opposite.

Our collaboration stems also from the eagerness of my (Professor Balabkins) desire to help make available to economists, political scientists, diplomats, and the policy-makers of the world's poor countries the substance of Professor Aizsilnieks's study of Latvia's economic evolution. My own value premise is that a vigorous private sector is an essential and powerful fuel for the engine of economic growth. Government bureaucrats can build and run the material, human, and institutional infrastructures of a country to advantage, but the directly productive activities—industry and agriculture—must be afforded a maximum of open opportunity. In other words, the three infrastructures produce *public* goods and services, whereas the directly productive activities produce *private* goods. For the most part, public goods and services are provided *gratis* to the public but are paid for ultimately by the taxpayer. By contrast private goods and services, like Cadillacs and motion pictures, are paid for by the general public, the consumer. The one is the legitimate province of the bureaucrat; the other should be, in my opinion, the province of private enterprise. Given my value premise, confirmed for me by the facts disclosed in Professor Aizsilnieks's study, I went one step further. I examined our collaborative effort against the contemporary theory of entrepreneurship. The conclusions were sufficiently illuminating to induce us to append a chapter on entrepreneurship as a yardstick by which scholars and others may measure the validity of our conclusions concerning entrepreneurship as they examine the "statist" economies of the developing countries of today.

The first part of the present volume embraces chapters on Latvia's history, its rise to sovereignty, its infrastructure, its industry and agriculture, in short, its total economic background. They are designed to show the institutional milieu in which private initiative and entrepreneurship evolved. The second part analyzes how, in the given political, geographic, and social setting, a particular large, privately-owned firm came into being, and how its operations demonstrated various manifestations of entrepreneurial activity. If these pages analyze adequately, clearly, and realistically the nature and function of entrepreneurship in a small country, the aim of these authors will be achieved.

Arnolds Aizsilnieks, Stockholm, Sweden,

and

Nicholas Balabkins, Bethlehem, Pennsylvania, U.S.A.
Summer, 1974

Part I
THE SMALL COUNTRY

The Baltic States: Ground to Dust

To most Americans the mere mention of the Baltic Sea evokes the romantic picture of a large body of water in Northern Europe, surrounded by Denmark to the west, Sweden and Finland to the north, Germany and Poland to the south, and the Soviet Union to the southeast. Some might vaguely remember that in the interwar period three small sovereign states—Estonia, Latvia, and Lithuania—existed along the eastern shores of that sea, but that somehow during World War II those countries were dropped from membership in the comity of nations. Few recall that, in contrast to the rapid decolonization process after World War II, when scores of new countries emerged from various quarters of the former colonial empires of Great Britain, France, Belgium, and Holland, the Baltic states had already lost their sovereignty, and to this date have not regained it.

The incorporation of these sovereign Baltic states into the Soviet Union as "republics" is one of the vexing and unresolved issues of post-1945 Europe. Moreover, the hopeful mood of a big-power detente in the early 1970s, the trend toward stabilization, or even legalization of the existing lines of political demarcation in Europe is even more likely to freeze the status quo. "Temporary arrangements" have a tendency to become cast in cement, and the wishes of the weak, who have no voice, carry no weight in the councils of the mighty. Yet, the Baltic nations have never forgotten that they have lost their sovereignty.

The Baltic States have remained largely *terra incognita*.[1] At the end of World War I, for instance, the general ignorance about Baltic Europe was truly astounding. For example, Colonel Stephen Tallents, who served in the British Mission in Latvia under General Sir Hubert Gough, was allowed to draw over one thousand "yen" for expenses. And, when he questioned the exchangeability of this oriental currency along the Baltic coast, he discovered that the ignorant official who had made out the order had supposed Latvia to be a Japanese island.[2]

Twenty years later the situation in the Baltic was still not much better, and one author felt compelled to note that the Asian Far East was generally better known than the borderlands of Eastern Europe.[3] When, in 1940, the three Baltic countries disappeared from the map of Europe, most of the people in Western Europe hardly knew why or how. One Englishman reported that to the vast majority of the British people "the Baltic had been for many years an unknown region."[4]

Regrettably, not much has been heard about Estonia, Latvia, and Lithuania in Western mass media since their forcible subsumption into the Soviet Union. The newly born sovereign countries, such as Burundi in East Africa, Sierra Leone in West Africa, Yemen in the southern part of Saudi Arabia, and Cyprus and Malta in the Mediterranean, have received more public attention than all three republics—Estonia, Latvia, and Lithuania —which continue to exist *de jure,* on paper, whereas *de facto* they have been forcibly absorbed into the Soviet Union. Is this a coincidence? Is it ignorance? Or, is it a "conspiracy of silence"[5] that has relegated the problem of the Baltic states to the dustbin of history?

The story of the rise and fall of the three Baltic states has not been entirely neglected. Told in a number of volumes, some of the accounts have been written by Baltic emigré scholars, former politicians and functionaries, and some have been penned even by native-born Americans and Englishmen. But, to the public at large, the fate of Baltic countries on the crossroads between two different civilizations—with the exception of that of Finland—remains either nebulous or neglected. Accordingly, a short historical sketch may prove useful, even though it may seem gratuitous to concerned readers with a stake in Baltic freedom.

Estonia, Latvia, and Lithuania lie on the eastern shores of the Baltic Sea. During its years of independence (1918-1940), Latvia had common borders with Estonia on the north, the Soviet Union on the east, Poland and Lithuania on the south, and the Baltic

Sea on the west. Latvia's territory of some 25,000 square miles corresponds roughly in size to West Virginia. Its population was almost two million in 1939. Latvia's Baltic neighbors were of comparable size, and relations with both were friendly, but not close enough to form a Baltic common market, or an economic or political union.[6]

A great opportunity to effect such a union existed at the time of the Baltic conference at Bulduri, in 1920, attended also by Poland and Finland. Had it been realized, it would have created a United States of the Baltic.[7] But the bitter dispute between Lithuania and Poland over Vilno destroyed that early hope for ever. From then on, the three small countries shifted for themselves, so to speak, practicing *Alleingang*, or a go-it-alone policy.

True enough, in 1923, Latvia concluded a temporary agreement for an economic and customs union with Estonia.[8] And for many years thereafter, numerous Latvian-Estonian committees worked on the necessary preliminaries leading toward implementation of their hoped-for economic union. The agreement's ultimate aim was to regulate the customs practices of the two countries, while also bringing into conformity all laws governing state monopolies, taxes and excise duties, transportation rates, labor legislation, and existing commercial arrangements with other countries.

Although the onset of the Great Depression brought this promising economic dialogue to a halt, it had already been considerably strained by the conclusion of the Soviet-Latvian commercial treaty of 1927. In fact, one perceptive historian felt that the "Latvian-Soviet commercial treaty made the materialization of the proposed Estonian-Latvian customs union next to impossible."[9]

Indeed, Latvia had made greater reductions in customs duties for Soviet goods than those proposed for the postulated Latvia-Estonia union. Estonians rightfully feared that the Latvians, by signing this treaty, had actually paved the way for making Estonia economically dependent on the Soviet Union.

In the depression gloom, all countries had turned busily to erecting high tariff walls, devaluating currencies, going off the gold standard, and introducing foreign exchange controls.

Estonia devalued its currency in June 1933, but Latvia did not and chose to retain the old parity up to 1936. Progress toward the customs union was never resumed and both countries remained economically separate entities.

Given the worldwide depression, these two small nations found themselves compelled by circumstances to practice near-autarchy. Even though their crossroads-like geographic position demanded that they cooperate in order to survive, they failed to do so. In retrospect, it seems that the end of these Latvian-Estonian talks was exactly what the two interested parties, the Soviet Union and Germany, desired.

Poland's seizure of Vilno made good relations with Lithuania impossible. Estonia and Latvia wanted friendly relations with Poland, as the largest of the *cordon sanitaire* states in Eastern Europe. But Lithuania nourished "its displeasure at the loss of its traditional capital, remained aloof and was to a certain degree inclined to be more kindly disposed to the Soviet Union, which had recognized its claim to the city."[10]

As long as the ancient Roman dictum of "divide and conquer" was ably practiced by both the Soviet Union and Germany, Baltic economic and political union remained a fantasy. And as long as the Soviet Union and Germany were weak, the small Baltic countries could practice neutralism in their foreign policy. In other words, neutralism is viable as long as the large powers remain weak. But all this changes when the large powers become or feel strong, as they did in 1939, when the Soviet Union and Nazi Germany concluded an agreement at the expense of the third parties.

It was precisely this danger to which the Report of the Royal Institute of International Affairs alluded in 1938 by noting that the three Baltic states ". . . are as much the potential battlefield for a clash between these two great ideological protagonists as they are the potential victims of agreement between them for their partition."[11] Like small peppercorns, Estonia, Latvia and Lithuania were ground into dust by the huge stones of the grist mill of European politics.

When, in 1920, the Soviet Union signed peace treaties with the three newly formed Baltic republics, it recognized "forever" their independence and sovereignty. The territorial losses that the brand new Soviet state had suffered by signing the various peace treaties—at a time when it was facing Allied intervention, internal chaos, and civil war—were negligible. The total land area of the Tsarist Empire in 1913 was approximately 22.3 million square kilometers, with a population of 165.7 million. The territory it ceded amounted to about one *thirty-seventh* of its land areas.[12] Yet it lost *one-sixth* of its former population, and, because it came from the most highly industrialized parts of the former Tsarist Empire, the Soviet Union only grudgingly accepted the loss of the Baltic provinces.

Not surprisingly, therefore, by 1924 the Soviet Union had supported a Communist-staged uprising in Estonia, while three Red Army divisions waited in readiness behind the frontier.[13] The Estonians, however, quickly and efficiently put down this insurrection. Relations between the two states were eventually formally repaired, but to Estonians the bad taste abided.

Latvia's relations with the USSR were difficult from the outset of independence;[14] friendly economic or political ties were virtually impossible. Before World War I, Latvia was already recognized as the most industrialized part of the huge Russian Empire. A number of factors combined to make this rapid industrialization possible: a favorable geographic location; the availability in Riga of an experienced business community, well connected with Western Europe; a high level of technological know-how; a well-developed banking community; an ongoing free-enterprise system; government protection of infant industries; the availability of numerous landless but literate Latvian peasants, and the construction of the Riga-Daugavpils-Saint Petersburg-Warsaw railroad.[15]

In short, Riga was not only a major port but also the hub of industrial and banking activity.[16]

Machine-making was particularly well developed in Latvia, as were production of chemicals and textiles, food-processing, and woodworking. During the war, most of the machinery was either evacuated to Russia or destroyed. According to one account, some 30,000 railroad cars were used to denude Riga of its industrial machinery.[17] When independence was achieved,

Latvia was in a shambles. The usually careful and reliable London *Economist* reported that "the country [had] suffered from the war even more severely than Belgium; it urgently needs foreign credits and foreign capital, the latter for advances, through a Land Bank, to agriculturists, to revive industry, to improve railways and harbours, and to support the State Bank."[18]

Latvian industry had also lost Russia's vast markets, and it was this loss that was felt most acutely in the 1920s.[19] In an attempt to cope with this problem, Latvia, in 1927, signed a five-year commercial treaty with the Soviet Union.[20] The treaty stipulated that the Soviet Union would order 40 millions lats (or $8 million) worth of goods from Latvia each year, and Latvia, in turn, would purchase from the Soviet Union 19 million lats (almost $4 million) worth of such items as oil, gasoline, sugar, iron, tobacco, and salt. The Soviet Union also committed itself to purchase Latvian-made railroad cars, woolen yarns, bicycles, agricultural machinery, textiles, purebred animals, and clover-seed. However, the ink was hardly dry when it became obvious that the Soviets had signed the treaty not so much for economic as for political reasons.[21] All members of the Soviet commercial mission in Riga enjoyed diplomatic immunity,[22] and they used this privilege to a full extent. Even the Latvian foreign minister, under whose auspicies the agreement was negotiated, wrote many years later in his memoirs that "such a treaty with the Soviet Union could in a way become dangerous to Latvia, if its President or Foreign Minister were Communist sympathizers or simple-minded ninnies, who kowtowed and cringed."[23]

To fulfill the annual Soviet orders, a number of Latvian firms had to expand their capacity, which called for a substantial outlay of funds. But it soon became obvious that the flow of Soviet orders was highly irregular, so that no firm could ever be sure whether it would receive orders for the next year. This on-and-off pattern of placing industrial orders repeatedly forced numerous firms in various industries to lay off part of their labor force and to reduce operations. The employers, who had no control over the situation, obviously did not make as much money as they had initially hoped.

By 1932, the full impact of the Great Depression had hit

Latvia. By that time Great Britain had lifted her economic boycott of the Soviet Union and had begun to import Russian timber and other products at the expense of England's former Latvian suppliers. The Latvian economy deteriorated considerably. To make matters worse, the commercial treaty with the Soviet Union expired in 1932. At the end of 1933, Latvia concluded another commercial treaty with the USSR, but its scope was much more limited. By 1934, Latvian exports to the Soviet Union were one-seventh of what they had been in 1932.[24]

The economic experience of the 1927 commercial treaty would tend to suggest that the Soviet Union did not need the Latvian ports as much as has often been claimed. This early example of Soviet treaty-making seems to make clear that the Russians were seeking political and ideological gains first, and that all other considerations were secondary.[25] It also serves to demonstrate how skillfully the Soviet Union uses such treaties for its own purposes. A number of similar agreements were signed after the first and second world wars, but the signatory governments appear not to have realized, or not to have scrutinized the provisions of the various paragraphs carefully enough to grasp, that they could only be net-losers.

For instance, the 1927 Soviet-Latvian commercial treaty called for substantial reciprocal reductions of import duties. The reduction of import duties on Soviet goods meant a considerable reduction of revenue to Latvia's treasury, whereas for the Soviets it meant that they could earn higher profits for their goods in Latvia than in other countries where they did not enjoy such favorable customs treatment.[26] Moreover, in the Soviet Union, all foreign trade was conducted by a state monopoly, which also supplied the economy with imported commodities at a fixed price. Lower import duties on Latvian goods meant, of course, lower revenue to the Soviet State Treasury, but since prices of goods remained fixed, the foreign trade monopoly made more money by getting Latvian goods at a lower duty. Since both institutions were a part of the Soviet government, this commercial treaty clearly was advantageous only to the USSR.

Thus, for some twenty years, the three Baltic states led a precarious existence wedged between two great powers. Yet they remained separate economic and political entities. As long as Soviet Russia was weak and Weimar Germany torn by parliamentary squabbles within the Reichstag, the burden of reparations, and the rising Nazi party, they were not threatened. Striving to remain outside the play of power politics, the Baltic countries became virtual addicts of neutralism and relied on the Covenant of the League of Nations for their protection.[27] But once the Soviet Union had consolidated its power and once Hitler had seized power in Germany, that hope faded because the League was too impotent to enforce that guarantee and protect the Baltic states.

With the outbreak of World War II, the position of the Baltic states became difficult in the extreme. Once Hitler decided to attack Poland, he wanted reassurance that the Soviet Union would be on his side. Toward this end he suggested to Stalin the establishment of their respective spheres of influence in Eastern Europe by signing the Nazi-Soviet Non-Aggression Pact of August 23, 1939.[28] Hitler, in his turn, promised not to interfere with Soviet policy in Eastern Poland and Estonia and Latvia. Some thirty-five years later the American diplomat Charles E. Bohlen made the following entry on that Soviet-Nazi agreement:

> Actually, it was Nazi power and the consequences of non-agreement with Germany that impelled Stalin to go ahead and sign the pact. He did not want Hitler to take all of Poland and have the panzer divisions that much closer to Moscow. Besides, Ribbentrop had given him almost everything he asked, and if all went well, the Soviet Union was assured of an indefinite period of peace. On paper, the Soviets seemed to have got a sphere of influence over the eastern part of Poland and over the Baltic states and Bessarabia, and the Germans got virtually nothing in the territorial sense except what they would fight for. What the Germans did get that was vital to them, however, was the avoidance of a war on two fronts.[29]

The spheres of influence were detailed in the *secret protocols* of the Nazi-Soviet Non-Aggression Pact, also signed on August 23, 1939.[30] What Hitler gave to the Soviet Union was not his to bestow. (Ironically, President Roosevelt, too, was "magnanimous" at the expense of Estonia, Latvia, and Lithuania. On

December 1, 1943, at the Tehran conference, he "jokingly" remarked to Stalin that when the Red Army reoccoupied the Baltic countries, Roosevelt "did not intend to go to war." [Robert Beitzell, *The Uneasy Alliance: America, Britain, and Russia, 1941-1943*, New York, Alfred A. Knopf, 1972, p. 346.] But Nazi Germany and the Soviet Union were big fish in the international waters at that time, whereas the Baltic states were not. Big fish eat small fish, Shakespeare once observed. For big powers there seems to be nothing immoral about making agreements at the expense of third parties. Surely, the two signatories were flagrantly violating international law, but the destruction of Baltic states was apparently simply accepted as a necessity of what is known as "great power politics."

Some five weeks later, on September 29, Estonia was compelled to sign a mutual assistance pact with the Soviet Union; Latvia did so on October 5, and Lithuania on October 11.[31] Under the terms of these treaties, the Soviet Union acquired naval and air bases in the three countries. All three "protective assistance" pacts contained "an article which expressly states that the internal organization of 'neither state' shall not be affected by what has transpired."[32] The *Economist* saw this as a grandiose gesture to placate world opinion. On the surface, the three republics continued to lead a sovereign existence, although with the outbreak of hostilities in September 1939, their position became extremely precarious. The German blockade of the Baltic Sea ruined their foreign trade, at the same time as the establishment of Soviet garrisons on their territories was immobilizing their little armies. Politically, they succumbed to a drift of "no-policy," trying not to offend either the Third Reich or the Soviet Union. The *Economist* noted that the Baltic states "pray for the downfall of both, but are powerless at the moment to do more than pray."[33]

Even though the contracting parties observed the mutual assistance pact scrupulously, the stationing of large contingents of Soviet military forces in the three Baltic republics created a major morale problem for the USSR. The *Economist* observed that "The sight of unlimited supplies of good, fresh food in the shops; footwear and clothing, obtainable without difficulty at

reasonable prices; and the general well-being of the people—
these are in such striking contrast with conditions in Russia that
even the most ardent disciples of Lenin and Marx must be
wondering what has gone wrong with The Great Experiment."[34]

This danger of "contamination" did not last for too long,
however. While the entire world watched the defeat of France
in June 1940, the Soviet Union—which had amassed some 120
divisions on its western borders—that same month entered the
three Baltic republics, thus completing the implementation of
some of the provisions of the Nazi-Soviet Non-Aggression Pact
of August 23, 1939. Outnumbered and outflanked, their armies
neutralized by the Soviet garrisons, their governments helpless
to act, their people hoping that the Soviets were not so bad after
all (at least not as bad as they had been in 1919), the three
republics did not offer any armed resistance to the Red Army.
Thus were three more nations crushed out of existence, like
Austria, Poland, the Low Countries, France, and Czechoslovakia
before them. By July, Estonia, Latvia, and Lithuania had lost
their independence "of their own free will." It was reported that
the act of giving up independence was staged in all three countries "on the same day and in the same way."[35] Even the
speeches delivered for the occasion had nearly identical wording.

The incorporation of the three Baltic states into the Soviet
Union established her superiority in the Eastern Baltic and added
some eight hundred miles of northern coastline and several
important military bases. After the destruction of these three
states, the *Economist* sadly noted that England had entered
World War II to check Hitler's aggression, to make restitution,
and to fight the battle of the rights and liberties of Europe. But
noting that Stalin had virtually crushed the Baltic states, it went
on to ask by "what strange political alchemy do these rights and
liberties disappear when the aggressor comes from the East?"[36]

The Nazi-Soviet Non-Aggression Pact, which had doomed
the Baltic states, was made null and void by the outbreak of
Russian-German hostilities on June 22, 1941; but in the
Soviet Union, the *secret protocols* of August 23, 1939, and the
supplement of September 28, 1939, which assigned Lithuania to
the Soviet Union, are still secret.[37] They have become something

like Orwellian "un-documents." Yet, incredible as it may seem, the political conditions that prevail in Estonia, Latvia, and Lithuania some thirty-five years later were created by the Soviet-Nazi pact, and this status quo remains virtually unchallenged today. De-colonization has reached into Africa and Asia, but it has not yet disturbed the intactness of the Soviet Empire.

As World War II broke out, the *Economist* wrote that the "Baltic States might by now have been making a more tangible contribution towards the establishment of a better European order *if they had in September the courage to act decisively as a unit* and to be less concerned with the individual privileges and political jobs. No matter what fate is now in store for Germany and Russia, the Baltic States in the long run will survive—if at all—only as a single economic and monetary unit. Their present military forces, though useless, are a heavy burden on the economic development of the three States. There will surely be no place in a better Europe for a cluster of independent, chauvinistic States in Eastern Europe that are more or less the private preserves of political cliques."[38]

It was a pious hope and a noble sermon. Today, with clear hindsight, we know that even if Poland and the three Baltic states had acted in unison, in defense and in foreign policy matters, they would not have been able to survive as independent states once the Soviet Union and Nazi Germany decided to crush them. Nobody would have come to their assistance under any circumstances in June of 1940. France was defeated, and England was staggering under the Dunkirk syndrome and Churchill's promise of nothing ahead but "Blood, Toil, Tears, and Sweat."

NOTES

1. L. W. Henderson, "Preface," in *Res Baltica: A Collection of Essays in Honor of the Memory of Dr. Alfred Bilmanis, 1887-1948*, edited by Adolf Sprudzs and Armins Rusis (Leyden: A. W. Sijthoff, 1968), p. 8 (hereafter cited as *Res Baltica*).

2. S. Tallents, *Man and Boy* (London: Faber & Faber, 1943), p. 261.

14 *Entrepreneur in a Small Country*

3. V. Zinghaus, *Führende Köpfe der baltischen Staaten:
31 Porträts*, (Kaunas: Ostverlag der Buchhandlung Pribacis,
1938), p. V.

4. W. F. Reddaway, *Problems of the Baltic* (Cambridge:
The University Press, 1940), p. 3.

5. I. Kavass and A. Sprudzs (editors), *Baltic States: A
Study of their Origin and National Development: Their Seizure
and Incorporation into the USSR*, Third Interim Report of the
Select Committee on Communist Aggression, House of Representatives, 83d Congress, 2d Session, 1954; *Reprint* (Buffalo,
New York: William S. Hein and Co., 1972), p. 2 (hereafter cited
as *Communist Aggression Report*).

6. E. Anderson, "Towards the Baltic Union, 1927-1934,"
Lituanus, vol. 12, no. 2 (1966), pp. 5-28; E. Anderson,
"Towards the Baltic Union, 1920-1927," *Lituanus*, vol. 13, no. 1
(1967), pp. 30-56; and by the same author, "Toward the Baltic
Union: The Initial Phase," *Lituanus*, vol. 14, no. 1 (1968), pp.
17-39.

7. A. Bilmanis, *Baltic Essays* (Washington, D.C.: Latvian
Legation, 1945), p. 15.

8. J. Volmars, *Europäische Zusammenarbeit und die Europäische Zollunion* (Braunschweig: G. Westermann Verlag,
1949), pp. 76-84.

9. E. Anderson, "The USSR Trades With Latvia: The
Treaty of 1927," *Slavic Review*, vol. 21, no. 2 (1962), p. 316.

10. C. A. Manning, *The Forgotten Republics* (New York:
Philosophical Library, 1952), p. 154.

11. Royal Institute of International Affairs, *The Baltic States:
A Survey of their Political and Economic Structures and the
Foreign Relations of Estonia, Latvia, and Lithuania* (London:
Oxford University Press, 1938), p. 4 (hereafter cited as *Baltic
States*).

12. USSR, *Narodnoe Khozaistvo SSR v 1963 godu* (Moscow,
1965), p. 7.

13. A. Rei, *The Drama of the Baltic Peoples* (Stockholm:
Publishing House Kirjastus Veba Eesti, 1970), p. 183.

14. E. Anderson, "The Role of the Baltic States between the

USSR and Western Europe," in *East European Quarterly*, vol. 7, no. 4 (1973), pp. 382-384.

15. M. I. Kozin (editor), *Ocherki Ekonomicheskoi Istorii Latvii, 1860-1900* (Riga: Zinātne, 1972), p. 108.

16. W. Lenz, *Die Entwicklung Rigas zur Grossstadt* (Kitzingen am Main: Holzner Verlag, 1954).

17. E. Bulmerinks, "Rīgas rūpniecība," in *Riga kā Latvijas galvas pilsēta* (Rīga: Rīgas pilsētas valdes izdevums, 1932), p. 130.

18. *The Economist*, vol. 95 (1922), p. 390.

19. J. A. Swettenham, *The Tragedy of the Baltic States* (London: Hollis and Carter, 1952), p. 52.

20. United Kingdom, Department of Overseas Trade, *Economic and Industrial Conditions in Latvia, May, 1929* (London: HMSO, 1929), p. 13.

21. Anderson, *op. cit.*, p. 317.

22. *Ibid.*, p. 307.

23. F. Cielēns, *Laikmetu mainā*, vol. 2 (Stockholm: Memento, 1963), p. 337.

24. A. Aizsilnieks, *Latvijas Saimniecības Vēsture, 1914-1945* (Stockholm: Daugava, 1968), p. 554 and p. 798.

25. Anderson, *op. cit.*, p. 321.

26. Soviet transit goods were carried by the Latvian railroads at freight rates which covered only the variable costs, i.e., wages and materials. Since Latvian ports in the 1920s were operating at only one-third their prewar level, it is conceivable that the Cielens government made very substantial economic concessions. See J. Rungis, "Latvija kā transitzeme pagājušos desmit pastāvēšanas gados," in *Latvijas Republika Desmit Pastāvēšanas Gados* (Rīga, 1928), pp. 320-322.

27. "Baltic Trio," *The Economist*, vol. 135 (1939), p. 596.

28. E. Čeginskas, "Die Baltische Frage in den Grossmächteverhandlungen 1939," in *Commentationes Balticae*, vol. 12/13 (1967), p. 49.

29. C. E. Bohlen, *Witness to History, 1929-1969* (New York: W. W. Norton and Co., 1973), p. 84.

30. D. A. Loeber, *Diktierte Option: Die Umsiedlung der*

Deutsch-Balten aus Estland und Lettland, 1939-1941 (Neumünster; Karl Wachholtz Verlag, 1972), pp. 18-19. See also B. J. Kaslas (ed.), *The USSR-German Aggression Against Lithuania* (New York: Robert Speller and Sons, Publishers, Inc., 1973), pp. 111-112.

31. B. Meissner, *Die Sowjetunion, die Baltischen Staaten und das Völkerrecht* (Köln: Verlag für Politik und Wirtschaft, 1956), pp. 57-67.

32. *The Economist*, vol. 137 (1939), p. 45.

33. *The Economist*, vol. 137 (1939), p. 464.

34. *The Economist*, vol. 138 (1940), p. 100.

35. "The New Soviet Republics," *The Economist*, vol. 139 (1940), p. 122.

36. *The Economist*, vol. 137 (1939), p. 464.

37. V. Petrov, "The Nazi-Soviet Pact: A Missing Page in Soviet Historiography," in *Problems of Communism*, vol. 17 (1968), pp. 42-50

38. *The Economist*, vol. 137 (1939), p. 464.

II

Latvia: Some "Forgotten" History

When the question is raised why Latvians have survived as a nation, the answer seems to lie in the realm of geography and demography.[1] It is rooted also in other factors—such as language, a high level of literacy, and folklore. As a branch of the Baltic peoples who formed the northern tip of the borderlands of western civilization, the Latvians succeeded in retaining their identity first as a group of tribes with their own culture, under their own chiefs or other subsequent forms of alien rule, to an ultimate short period of true self-determination in the interwar period. Was it their borderland position, with the sea as a protective barrier? Or was it their ties of a commonality that enabled the Latvians to survive?

At the risk of belaboring the obvious, retelling the familiar, and offending certain economists, the story of the "forgotten republics" on the Baltic Sea may here be continued in further depth with focus on Latvia, for those who have forgotten or never knew the story.

As late as the thirteenth century, the Latvian people were divided into separate tribes. These were then conquered, either by defeat on the battlefield or by deceit by German knights. By the end of the thirteenth century Christianity was established in the territory and German knights were in control.[2] The subjugation of the Latvian tribes gave rise to a confederation known as the Livonian Church States.[3] With the passage of time, many of the German knights became landlords, who imposed upon Latvian peasants heavy mandatory obligations, mostly in edibles, and prescribed a set number of statute work days per year on the estates. After the great Black Death at the end of the fifteenth century had decimated the population, the remaining Latvian peasants were transformed into serfs, legally tied to their estates while the landlords became the sole owners of the land.

In the second half of the sixteenth century the Confederation of the Livonian Church States collapsed in the wake of Russian westward expansion.[4] Subsequently, various parts of the Latvian-populated territory were subjugated successively by Lithuania, Poland, Sweden and finally Russia. Livland, the northern part of the territory, was taken over by Russia in 1710 and, after the peace treaty of 1721, became formally known as part of the Livlandic Province. Lettgallia, the easternmost part, fell to Russia in 1772 to become part of the Vitebsk province. Lastly, the dukedom of Courland (Courland and Semgallia) was incorporated as a Russian province in 1795. Thus it was only in the late eighteenth century that Russia became a great power on the shores of the Baltic Sea.[5]

Upon the incorporation of Livland into Russia, its German landed gentry succeeded in obtaining a number of new privileges and rights. But with their administration of the province, the status of the Latvian peasant deteriorated to a point approaching slavery. Peasants owned nothing, they could be bought and sold, and they were punished, even put to death, according to the landlord's whim or judgment. The German landed gentry of Courland and Semgallia won similar privileges.

Conditions in Lettgallia, where the landed estates belonged primarily to Polish or German-turned-Polish landowners, were different. These landowners enjoyed neither the Russian government's support nor its trust because of the frequent uprisings in Poland.

Serfdom was finally abolished in Courland and Semgallia in 1817, and in Livland in 1819. The landowners, however, managed to write the law in such a way that the land remained in their hands, while the peasants obtained only "bird's freedom" without even the privilege of migrating from their provinces. "Liberated" former serfs were therefore compelled either to remain on estates as servants or to rent land from their land-owning masters. As a rule, the peasants had to pay their rent in farm products in addition to working a prescribed number of days on the estate fields, an extremely burdensome require-

ment. Consequently, Latvian peasants, bitterly disappointed
with the 1817 and 1819 laws, engaged in periodic uprisings.

It took about fifty years for the Russian government to
abolish statute work, introduce monetary rent payments, and
give the peasants even a chance to become small landowners
themselves. Serfdom was not abolished in Lettgallia until 1861,
by a decree that affected all of Russia. Russian "emancipated"
peasants were given shares of estate lands for long-term use. Because of peasant unrest in Poland and Lithuania, however, land
in Lettgallia was available for purchase only to clans that could
obtain long-term credits. Here the peasants lived in village-
like settlements. Until 1906, however, they could not erect
buildings outside the settlement without special permission. Individual peasants farmed not one piece of land, but long narrow
strips in different locations, which made efficient farming virtually impossible. Before World War I, 48 percent of the entire
Latvian territory was owned by 820 families; peasants owned
39 percent and the state owned 10 percent.[6] Unfriendly relations
between the landed gentry and the peasants frequently led to
peasant uprisings. The German-speaking landlords regarded
Latvian peasants as "white niggers."[7] This label reflected the
attitude of the former landowners to the first and second gener-
ation of freed serfs. The Baltic barons lived, felt, and acted
like the German *Herrenvolk*.[8]

In 1905, peasant unrest was particularly widespread. It
started with a revolt of workers in the cities and towns, went
on to turn into a full scale revolution, but was later suppressed
by Russian troops. After the revolution of 1905, German landowners tried to recruit Germans to replace their former Latvian
servants on the estates. In addition, in 1907 some German noble-
men set up a private organization that bought up heavily in-
debted estates and peasant farms to create homesteads for
colonists from Germany and thereby increase the number of
Germans in Latvia. By 1914 about 20,000 German colonists had
settled on Latvian territory. These colonists liked Latvia and
invited their relatives and other fellow-Germans to join them.[9]
At the same time, Russian administrators made efforts to Rus-

sianize the Latvians. In Lettgallia as early as 1865, they out-
lawed the Latin alphabet and required that all books be printed
in the Cyrillic alphabet. This decree was in force up to 1904.
In other parts of Latvia there were also attempts, largely un-
successful, to force Latvians to use Cyrillic characters.[10] Russian
agricultural banks, which provided long-term loans, regularly
bought up private estates for the purpose of settling Russian
peasants on them. The Russians also brought colonists to state-
owned estates, a substantial number of which were located in
Courland.[11]

During World War I, in 1915, German troops occupied all of
Courland and part of Semgallia. Shortly thereafter the German
authorities began preparing Courland for settlement by German
colonists. German landowners committed themselves to part
with one-third of their holdings for colonization. Furthermore,
numerous Latvian peasants who fled to Russia before the ad-
vancing German troops, or were evacuated, left their farms un-
tended, and these were taken over for the eventual new German
settlers. The colonizing agencies were given the first options
to buy whenever peasants' lands were to be sold, either voluntarily or at auction. Large sums were amassed to implement colonization, with the active participation of some of Germany's
largest industrial firms.[12] Only Germany's defeat in the war ended these plans.

Despite the deep-seated antagonism and social distance
between the Latvian peasants and the German-speaking landed
gentry, Latvian territory prior to the outbreak of World War I
already had a well-developed agriculture with a growing tendency towards dairy farming. Many Latvian peasants kept purebred cows and earned extra income from dairy farming (by
selling milk). By 1915 the Latvian peasantry had organized 88
dairy associations, most of them located in Livland. Active at
this time were 163 agricultural associations, 294 cattle-breeder's
associations, and about 150 agricultural (farm) machine-users'
cooperatives, all peasant-organized and peasant-run. These associations were all members of the Agricultural Central Association of Riga, the only institution of its kind in prewar Russia.
It employed qualified agronomists (specialists in farm and soil

management) and other farm specialists, who organized training courses for the peasants, offered advice, and kept cattle-
breeding books.[13]

Before World War I, Latvia also had a considerable industrial capacity, even by contemporary standards. In 1900, for
instance, 404 large industrial firms operating on Latvian territory
employed 60,636 workers.[14] Industrial growth continued at a
fast clip until, by 1913, 753 of the largest industrial firms employed 108,600 workers, of whom 87,800 worked in Riga. Industrial concentration was particularly pronounced in Riga. The
second largest industrial city in Latvian territory was Liepāja.
The industrial workers came either from the Latvian countryside or from Russia proper, and most of them were employed
in machine-building, rubber-working, and textiles. Raw materials and coal came either from abroad by ship or from Russia
by rail. The Latvian industrial output went to both the European and the vast Russian markets. The Baltic Railroad Car
Works of Riga had even started to produce automobiles, some
of which had been entered in international car races and had
on occasions won.[15]

The largest industrial enterprises and banks in Latvian territory at that time were controlled by Germany's financiers and
industrialists, although English and Belgian capital was invested
in a few firms as well. Almost all managers, engineers, and
technicians in the large firms were German.[16]

Riga was one of the most important ports of the vast Russian
Empire prior to World War I. Through it Russia shipped a
large portion of her exports. During the five-year period from
1896 to 1900, Riga accounted for 19 percent of Russia's exports,
14 percent of imports, and 16.6 percent of the total trade volume
(imports and exports combined).[17] In 1913, Riga's share of the
total trade volume of all Russian ports was 17.2 percent, whereas Petersburg, now Leningrad, accounted for 14 percent. And
together, all the Latvian ports (Riga, Liepaja, Ventspils) accounted for a considerably higher proportion of Russia's foreign
trade. In 1913, Latvian ports shipped 28.6 percent of all Russian
exports and accounted for 24.5 percent of the total trade volume
of all Russian ports.[18]

In 1915 the German Army occupied Courland; in 1917, Riga; and in the early part of 1918, Livland. In November 1917 the Russian Bolshevik party made a successful bid for power. A few months later, on March 3, 1918, Lenin's government signed the Brest-Litovsk peace treaty with Germany, under the terms of which Soviet Russia ceded Courland to Germany. Later on, a special provision stipulated that Soviet Russia was also to cede Livland and retain only Lettgallia, the easternmost part of Latvia.[19] Under the terms of this treaty Lenin's government signed away Poland, the Ukraine, the Baltic provinces, and other border areas inhabited by non-Russians. The Bolsheviks had pledged to the war-weary Russians that they would end the war as soon as possible, so that the prospects of peace made bearable the loss of so much territory.

But the Brest-Litovsk peace did not last long; for on November 8, 1918, a revolution broke out in Germany, and the German surrender on November 11 ended World War I. Although the Western Powers did not recognize the peace treaty of Brest-Litovsk, nor Germany's annexation of Latvian territory, their November 11 Armistice terms required that the Germans make a gradual withdrawal from the entire Baltic territory. They were ordered to remain there as long as the Western powers felt it necessary to protect the Baltic territory from the Bolshevik army.[20] However, Germany ignored this part of the Armistice and withdrew its army from the Baltic provinces shortly thereafter, leaving the Latvian territory without protection.

The Wilsonian slogan of self-determination was on everybody's lips at that time, and Latvians were no exception. They wanted to be rulers of their own land, and not to kowtow either to German landlords or Russian bureaucrats.

On November 17, 1918, the Latvian National Council came into being and a day later they proclaimed a sovereign and democratic republic of Latvia.[21] A month later, however, the Russian Bolshevik party formed a Latvian Soviet government, and sent armed forces towards Latvia. On January 3, 1919, the Red Army, including among others Red Latvian troops, entered Riga.[22] The rest of Latvia, except for a small part of Courland, also fell before the Soviet forces, which finally stopped near Liepāja around January 20, 1919.[23]

Although the German occupation authorities allowed the Latvian National Committee to proclaim the independence of Latvia on November 18, 1918, they did not permit the newly formed Latvian government to decree mobilization or to raise any armed forces. Under such circumstances the Latvian government had no choice but to flee to Liepāja. At about the same time, volunteer troops organized by the local landed gentry went to Courland. Some of these troops succeeded in forcing the provisional government of Latvia to seek refuge on the ship *Saratov,* under Allied protection. By that time the Baltic Sea was already controlled by the mighty British Navy.[24] The stagers of this coup d'etat formed their own government, which was favorably disposed towards Baltic Germans.

On May 22, 1919, the military units of the Baltic Germans, together with Latvian volunteers, liberated Riga from the Soviets. Shortly thereafter the Baltic German forces attacked the Estonian and Latvian military units, which had been formed in northern Latvia, but they were defeated and forced to retreat to Courland. By June, however, the Latvian government formed by the landed gentry in Liepāja resigned, and the provisional government returned to Riga.[25]

Subsequently, the Baltic German military forces, anticommunist Russian volunteer units, and volunteer units recruited in Germany with promises of land in the Baltic countries after the war, formed a new army under the command of the Russian adventurer, Colonel Bermondt, or Prince Avalov, Bermondt-Avalov.[26] The leaders of this military force hoped eventually to fight the Bolsheviks in Russia. In October 1919, while Latvian troops were fighting Soviet troops in Lettgallia, the army of Bermondt-Avalov attacked Riga. Quickly formed Latvian military units successfully repelled this attack, so that by the end of November the attackers were driven out of Latvian territory.[27]

The plan to provide the German volunteers of the Bermondt-Avalov army with land in Latvia had been a carefully worked-out colonization venture. The local landed gentry had agreed to part with one-third of their estates for such purposes. The soldiers were divided into groups, each of which was provided a particular estate. Every group had its village association, which, in turn, was a member of a larger association, called the

Soldier's Settlement Association of Courland (Soldaten Siedlungs-
Verband Kurland).[28] In this way the Latvian volunteer troops,
by defeating the army of Bermondt-Avalov, also destroyed the
German plan for colonizing Latvia.

Not until 1920 did the Latvian armed forces clear the country
of the invading Germans and Russians. Only then could the
provisional government of Latvia begin the reconstruction and
rehabilitation of the country's devastated economy. In the peace
treaty with Latvia, the Soviet Union declared that it recognized,
without reservation, the independence and sovereignty of the
Latvian Republic.

NOTES

1. M. Gimbutas, *The Balts* (London: Thames and Hudson,
1963), pp. 21-36; and S. K. Chatterji, *Balts and Aryans in their
Indo-European Background* (Simla, India: Institute of Advanced
Study, 1968).

2. A. Rei, *The Drama of the Baltic Peoples* (Stockholm:
Publishing House Kirjastus Vaba Eesti, 1970), chapter one, "The
Baltic Nations Through Millennia," pp. 11-37; see also R. Wit-
tram, *Baltische Geschichte* (München: Verlag R. Oldenbourg,
1954), pp. 16-28.

3. A. Bilmanis, "The Struggle for Domination of the Baltic,"
Journal of Central European Affairs, vol. 5 (1945-46), pp. 119-
142.

4. W. Kirchner, *The Rise of the Baltic Question* (Newark,
Delaware: University of Delaware Press, 1954), p. 254.

5. G. V. Rauch, *Geschichte der baltischen Staaten*
(Stuttgart: W. Kohlhammer Verlag, 1970), p. 14.

6. J. Birznieks, "Latvian Agriculture in the Past Twenty
Years," *The Latvian Economist,* 1938, pp. 40-41.

7. H. F. Anderson, *Borderline Russia* (London: The Cres-
set Press, 1942), p. 46.

8. S. W. Page, *The Formation of the Baltic States: A Study
of the Effects of Great Power Politics upon the Emergence of
Lithuania, Latvia, and Estonia* (Cambridge, Mass.: Harvard
University Press, 1959), p. 10.

9. A. Švābe, *Latvijas vēsture, 1800-1914* (Stockholm: Daugava, 1958), p. 670.

10. *Ibid.*, p. 302.

11. *Ibid.*, p. 671.

12. A. Aizsilnieks, *Latvijas saimniecības vēsture, 1914-1945* (Stockholm: Daugava, 1968), pp. 63-68 (hereafter cited as *Aizsilnieks*).

13. Švābe, *op. cit.*, pp. 695-96.

14. M. I. Kozin (ed.), *Ocherki ekonomicheskoi istorii Latvii, 1860-1900* (An Outline of Economic History of Latvia, 1860-1900) (Rīga: Zinātne, 1972), p. 373.

15. Švābe, *op. cit.*, p. 685.

16. *Ibid.*, p. 695.

17. Kozin, *op. cit.*, p. 481.

18. Švābe, *op. cit.*, p. 689.

19. M. Bobe, S. Levenberg, I. Maor, Z. Michaeli (editors), *The Jews in Latvia* (Tel-Aviv: Association of Latvian and Estonian Jews in Israel, 1971), p. 49.

20. A. Spekke, *History of Latvia: An Outline* (Stockholm: M. Goppers, 1951), pp. 342-343 and p. 346.

21. E. Andersons, *Latvijas vēsture, 1914-1920* (Stockholm: Daugava, 1967), pp. 352-366; and J. V. Hehn, "Die Gründung der Republik im Jahre 1918," *Zeitschrift für Ostforschung*, vol. 18 (1969), pp. 723-732.

22. Page, *op. cit.*, p. 135.

23. Andersons, *op. cit.*, pp. 367-383; see also Spekke, *op. cit.*, p. 347.

24. H. A. G. Watson, *The Latvian Republic: The Struggle for Freedom* (London: George Allen & Unwin, 1965), p. 86; see also S. Tallents, *Man and Boy* (London: Faber & Farber, 1943), pp. 278 and 281.

25. Andersons, *op. cit.*, pp. 427-455.

26. Watson, *op. cit.*, p. 72.

27. Aizsilnieks, p. 108.

28. *Ibid.*, pp. 148-149.

III

The Latvian Infrastructure
in the 1920s

After the end of hostilities in 1920 the Latvian infrastructure, or what the professional economist calls *social overhead capital,* was almost completely destroyed. For the noneconomist, the term may bear elucidation. The concept of infrastructure is usually divided into the three categories of *material, human,* and *institutional.*[1]

Material infrastructure consists of roads, railways, communications systems, irrigation facilities, gas and electricity generating and transmitting networks, ports, airports, sewers, and so on. At times material infrastructure is also called capital-intensive infrastructure.[2] The existence and sound operating condition of these facilities is indispensable for the successful operation of industry and agriculture. By themselves roads and canals produce nothing that is readily edible, potable, or wearable on one's back, but without roads and canals the farmer and industrial producer could hardly deliver his finished produce to the market or obtain raw materials for production. Again, the economist would say that without the existence of a well-functioning material infrastructure, *directly productive activities* of industry and agriculture (i.e., those producing ready-made goods) would be impossible.[3]

The second component of the infrastructure or social overhead capital, the human infrastructure, generally refers to the population of working age, its education, initiative-taking ability, or adaptability to change, nutrition, health, mortality, and fertility. Primary, secondary, and vocational education, the presence or absence of competent and motivated teachers and students alike, universities, and ongoing research are also components of human infrastructure and are indispensable for the sustained evolution of a country.[4] The nation's health includes such basic matters as the incidence of disease—tuberculosis, malaria, beri-beri, snail fever, yellow fever, hookworm, dysentery, trachoma, among many others—and of malnutrition (i.e., inadequate protein intake). Again, although high or low levels of educational achievement and good and or bad health, do not produce anything by themselves, a literate, healthy, and well-fed population constitutes the *development potential* of a country. This part of infrastructure can also be called the *brain power* of a country. Without it, wealth can be neither created nor re-created and its absence affects negatively industry and agriculture.[5] A country without sufficient brain power is reflected in low output per man, machine, or ox. In a war-ravaged country like Latvia after 1920, it represented *recuperational potential*.

The third integral component, institutional infrastructure,[6] consists of the legislative process and the legal framework (contracts, property rights, inheritance laws and so on), law enforcement (or lack of it through a permissive judiciary), and social phenomena—habits, customs, mores, traditions, the presence or absence of a caste system, social classes and social distance among classes, land tenure, local government, corruption, the presence or absence of a "work ethic," the existence of extended families, down to such details as the tendency of villagers to fear all strangers. To contemporary economists the concept of institutional infrastructure is too vague, not easily quantifiable, and thus not very meaningful. Therefore it is often dismissed as "unimportant." Yet, elusive as may be this third component of infrastructure, it represents in essence a nation's culture and must be considered important.

It is only in the last decade that economists have begun to relearn and rediscover through *direct observation* that noneconomic elements are responsible for stagnation in many parts of Asia, Africa, and Latin America. Despite the hundreds of billions of dollars in aid and grants that have flowed to the world's poor countries since the end of World War II from Europe and the United States, these countries have lingered in the "backwardness trap." Thus, although this complex institutional component of the infrastructure, like the other two components, does not by itself produce any wheat, rice, clothing, nails, or steel, it can facilitate or deter directly productive activities in industry and agriculture. Without institutional infrastructure, which cannot be created overnight—despite the roads, canals, sewers, ports, and telephones, which can be built rather rapidly —a country may continue to stagnate and not reach the so-called and hoped-for take-off stage into modernization. Growth and structural change, after all, result from an *interlock* of technological, organizational, and cultural components of economic behavior.[7]

The development of the material, human, and institutional infrastructure is a slow process, yet one which must take place in all three categories more or less simultaneously. Can underdeveloped countries create in decades what Europeans took almost a millennium to achieve? During economic development market forces must also develop, along with the monetization of production, division of labor, and purchase of inputs from other specialized producers. In short, to build a house one first needs a solid foundation. If one reasons by analogy and permits himself the luxury of oversimplification, the material, human, and institutional infrastructure constitute a foundation on which to build an economy. That is, the primary (mining and agriculture), secondary (industry), and tertiary industries (services) can be mounted upon it. This brief digression on the concept of infrastructure, or social overhead capital, is designed to emphasize its strategic role in economic change for the reader who has not encountered or dealt with this problem at first hand. The real world situations are, of course, too complex to conform exactly to the above neat and simple abstraction of reality. Today, scores of small and large developing countries strive to better their lot too quickly, without realizing that inadequate infrastructures can cripple their efforts.

Latvia's material infrastructure during World War I was so heavily damaged that it was practically nonexistent. All railroad bridges had been blown up, and the bulk of the locomotives and railroad cars had been taken either to Germany or Soviet Russia. Most of the railroad stations were in ruins and the railroad repair yards suffered from lack of equipment, machinery, and raw materials. The postal and telegraphic equipment had been evacuated to Russia near the beginning of the war, nor had the German authorities permitted restoration of the communications system during their occupation. The telephone system was destroyed as well. Country roads, well kept before the war for the horse-and-wagon traffic, were mostly impassable after the years of disrepair. Thousands of small bridges were gone as well. The country's ports had been either mined, destroyed, silted up, or blocked by sunken ships; the port cranes and warehouses had been either destroyed or damaged; and the Baltic Sea was still mined. In 1920, only 45 of 333 steamers and sailing vessels that had belonged to Latvian shipowners were left, and they were in poor repair. The long war had transformed the once prosperous countryside into a moonscape pitted with craters, transected by barbed-wire fences and trenches, and littered with abandoned fortifications.[8] By 1920 as much as one-fourth of the whole of Latvia still lay devastated.[9] The rest of the countryside had also suffered severely, as had the cities.[10]

Shortly after the outbreak of World War I, as mentioned earlier, the Russian government had evacuated to Russia the machinery and equipment of the largest industrial plants. Consequently, after the war, for many years to come in many cities, the plants stood empty and/or idle, moldering away. Similarly, numerous schools, hospitals, and administrative buildings and equipment had been destroyed.[11]

One of the leading Latvian statesmen, Margers Skujnieks, characterized the prevailing situation at the beginning of independence, as follows:

Of all European nations Latvia suffered the heaviest losses during the war. Relatively speaking even Belgium and France suffered less. In 1918 when Latvia proclaimed its sovereignty, its land had been destroyed, and plundered; it was depopulated and incredibly poor. For many years millions of soldiers had trampled our land. For many years in the very heart of Latvia, on the banks of river Daugava, stood the main battle line of the belligerents. Fire and brutal destructiveness continued to destroy Latvian farms and fields. In 1920, 72,278 farms lay in complete ruins, and 104,574 farm buildings, i.e., ¼ of all buildings in Latvia, had been partially destroyed. The richest regions of Latvia had been depopulated, and farm lands and orchards were taken over by weeds and brush.[12]

Because Latvia's human losses were staggering, its human infrastructure was badly impaired. Whereas in 1914, 2.6 million people had lived in Latvian territory, in June 1920, only 1.6 million were accounted for.[13] Many inhabitants had gone to Russia to escape from the war zone; numerous skilled workers and their families had left for Russia along with the evacuated machinery during the early days of the war. Many railroad workers, engineers, postal and telegraph workers, bank clerks, and government workers had gone never to return. In fact, roughly 200,000 Latvians were to remain in the Soviet Union.[14] The Russian Army had drafted the strongest and healthiest Latvian men, many of whom were either killed in action or returned home as invalids. The liberation of Latvia from the Red Army and the German forces also resulted in manpower losses. Population losses were actually the hardest to bear, for it deprived the country of much of its brainpower and muscle. Such a large reduction in the human capital of the new country drastically affected its recuperative and developmental potential. No one will ever be able to estimate the cost and value of the education and the professional training of those who died or were maimed or remained in the Soviet Union; these prewar outlays were simply lost. And, although the value of all machines, equipment, animals, and raw materials evacuated to Russia has been estimated from 1.3 billion lats[15] to 500 million (prewar) rubles,[16] Latvia eventually received back only 3.0 million lats' worth of machinery and equipment.[17] Machines, equipment, and supplies at least can be replaced rather quickly, but it would take generations to make up for the dreadful bloodletting of Latvia's human infrastructure. The new country felt the gap of missing men and women very much for a long time.

Latvia's institutional infrastructure—that is, such things as laws, courts, police, administration, social mores, and customs—had also been partially destroyed, and what was left did not function well in the new sovereign state. The British Consul in Riga, Mr. C. A. Edmond, reported that "the new State [had] to start almost *de novo*."[18] The new country was now completely detached from the Soviet Russian economic sphere, of which she had once been an integral part. Of the prevailing difficult economic conditions, the *London Economist* remarked caustically that "the only hope for economic reconstruction lies in a foreign loan. But the terms now would be onerous, if not prohibitive."[19] It quickly became obvious that the Soviet Union, with its new and specific social order, did not wish to renew the former economic ties with those newly independent states that were no longer part of Russia. For this reason it would have been foolish to restore the industrial structure according to the prewar pattern, because goods produced formerly for the Russians would have no markets. Thus Latvia had the two-fold problem of transforming not only its industrial structure but also its institutional infrastructure, which is a part of the political system.

The new republic quickly wrote a new constitution, which was accepted by the Constitutional Assembly in session from 1920 to 1922. This constitution declared Latvia an independent and sovereign republic with a democratic political system and all sovereign power resting with the Latvian people. But a constitution alone is not sufficient to govern a country. The entire judicial system, including the operations of courts and the civil codes, was due to be changed, a process that would have required many years. But because it was urgent that the country begin operating—to form the army, issue currency, finance indispensable imports, appoint ministers, and hire clerks—there was no time for slow evolutionary institutional change. Hence, as a matter of expediency, the Latvian National Council decided on December 5, 1919, to retain all Russian laws in force in Latvia, provided they had come into force prior to October 24, 1917, i.e., prior to the Communist accession to power. Thereafter the adaptation and changes of these Russian laws took many, many years.[20]

The Russian-trained and -educated Latvian officials felt at home in this judicial and administrative milieu, for they already knew how to run this kind of system.[21] In the early years of independence visiting Western journalists were struck by the similarities between prewar Russia and the new Baltic states.[22] After gaining independence Latvians filled the numerous posts in the material, human, and institutional infrastructure formerly occupied by Russians and Baltic Germans. This sudden upward mobility of the thousands led to wholesale emulation of the erstwhile occupiers of those bureaucratic posts, a situation very similar to that which took place in the 1950s and 1960s in Africa and Asia. The former underlings knew no alternative but to emulate the patterns of Russian bureaucracy. To the rest of lower strata Latvians, careers in bureaucracy became a socially desirable occupation. It was this detention of former Russian laws and legislative and administrative traditions that proved to be the most burdensome inheritance for the new Latvian republic, because it virtually forced Latvia's economic and social development back into the old Russian stereotype.[23] This is a process that we have seen repeated again and again in the developing nations of Africa and Asia, as they perpetuate the institutions of the former imperial powers that held them in colonial thrall.

NOTES

1. R. L. Frey, *Infrastruktur: Grundlagen der Planung öffentlicher Investitionen* (Tübingen: J. C. B. Mohr [Paul Siebeck], 1972), pp. 18-22. See also R. Jochimsen, *Theorie der Infrastruktur* (Tübingen: J. C. B. Mohr [Paul Siebeck], 1966), pp. 117-118, p. 100, and pp. 133-135; and E. Tuchtfeldt, "Infrastrukturinvestitionen als Mittel der Strukturpolitik," in *Theorie und Praxis der Infrastrukturpolitik*, edited by R. Jochimsen and U. E. Simonis (Berlin: Verlag von Duncker & Humbolt, 1970), pp. 125-145.

2. C. W. Wharton, "The Infrastructure for Agricultural Growth," in *Agricultural Development and Economic Growth*, edited by H. M. Southworth and B. F. Johnston (New York: Cornell University Press, 1967), p. 110 (hereafter cited as *Agricultural Development*).

3. The concept of *directly productive activities* was introduced into the literature by A. O. Hirschman, in his *The Strategy of Economic Development* (New Haven: Yale University Press, 1967), pp. 83-85.

4. G. Myrdal, *Asian Drama, An Inquiry Into the Poverty of Nations*, vol. 3 (New York: The Twentieth Century Fund, 1968); chapters 29-33 deal with such matters as 'Investment in Man,' Health, Education: the Legacy, Literacy and Adult Education, and The School System, pp. 1533-1828.

5. H. W. Singer, *International Development: Growth and Change* (New York: McGraw-Hill, 1964), p. 66.

6. Jochimsen, *op. cit., pp.* 117-118.

7. *Agricultural Development,* p. 70.

8. Aizsilnieks, pp. 134-136 and pp. 222-224.

9. M. Walters, in his *Lettland, seine Entwicklung zum Staat und die Baltischen Fragen* (Rome, 1923), states, for example, that in 1920, 30 percent of the agriculturally usable land in Livland lay idle; in Courland it was 50 and in Lettgallia 40 percent.

10. A. Zalts, *Latvian Political Economy* (Riga: The Riga Times Edition, 1928), p. 109.

11. E. Blanks, "Latvijas valsts sagatavošanas laikmets," in *Latvija Desmit Gados* (Rīga, Jubilejas Komisijas Izdevums, 1928), p. 11.

12. M. Skujnieks, *Latvija 1918-1928 gados* (Rīga, 1928), p. 3.

13. J. Rutkis, *Latvijas geografija* (Stockholm: Apgāds Zemgale, 1960), p. 268.

14. D. A. Loeber, "Latvian Emigres in the Soviet Union, 1919-1940," *Second Conference on Baltic Studies, Summary of Proceedings* (Norman, Oklahoma: Association for the Advancement of Baltic Studies, 1971), p. 61. This group was almost twice as large as the Latvian exodus during World War II, when some 110,000 people left the country. According to another source (Namsons, A., "Letten in der Sowjetunion und ihr materielles und kulturelles Leben," in *Acta Baltica*, vol. 11 [1971], p. 131), in 1926, 151,400 Latvians resided in the Soviet Union.

15. E. Bulmerinks, "Rīgas Rūpniecība," in *Rīga Kā Latvijas Galvas Pilsēta* (Rīga, Pilsētas Valdes Izdevums, 1932), p. 130.

34	*Entrepreneur in a Small Country*

16. K. Balodis, *Runas,* III Saeimas Sesijās, Aprīlī-Maijā, 1929 (Rīga: Spiestuve Izdevējs, 1930), p. 57.

17. *Latvija desmit gados* (Rīga, 1928), p. 66. See also Aizsilnieks, p. 163.

18. U.K. Department of Overseas Trade. *Economic and Industrial Conditions in Latvia, May, 1929* (London: HMSO, 1929), p. 7.

19. *The Economist,* vol. 94 (1922), p. 400.

20. A. Švābe (ed.), *Latvju Enciklopēdija* (Stockholm: Apgāds Trīs Zvaigznes, 1953-1955), p. 2444.

21. A good example was the Latvian Civil Law. See Carl v. Schilling and Herbert Ehlers, editors, *Lettlands Bürgerliches Gesetzbuch* (Riga: Verlag E. Plates, 1929), Teil III: des Provinzialrechts der Osteseegouvernements (Liv-und Kurländisches Privatrecht) nebst den russischen "Fortsetzungen" der Jahre 1890, 1912, 1913 un 1914, sowie den Abäderungen und Ergänzungen von Lettlands Begründung und bis zum 1. Oktober 1928, 646 pp.

22. For example, J., "Northern Europe After Fifteen Years," *The Spectator,* vol. 139 (1927): p. 495.

23. Aizsilnieks, p. 958.

IV

Seeds of Statism

From the very inception of independence, the evolution of Latvian economic life was marked by a trend towards state-owned and state-run enterprises, state monopolies, and augmentation of state-owned national wealth, such as land, forests, and minerals. Foremost among the numerous reasons for this early trend was the necessity to meet immediate needs during the War of Liberation and to take expedient steps to deal with the peculiar economic structure left upon the departure of the Soviet Latvian government. To begin with, as the Red Army troops retreated in mid-1919, the provisional government took over Soviet-created industrial enterprises and kept them running. To be sure, most of these production facilities were small, but the extreme shortages of consumer goods and industrial supplies made continued production necessary in order to meet the minimum needs of both the Latvian army and the populace. Under the prevailing wartime conditions, only state-appointed officials could assure continued functioning of the industrial sector. Hence the interim state system was one of pure expediency.

The acute shortages of war material and agricultural implements—together with the concomitant passivity of the private sector—was added impetus for state agencies to get involved in the economic affairs of the country. As long as the front lines had moved back and forth across the newly independent country, private businessmen had held back. For this reason, the national government quickly set up production facilities to manufacture indispensable military supplies, agricultural implements, and consumer goods.[1] To supervise all these diverse activities, in 1919 the new government created the Control Agency of Enterprises[2]

35

One of the first acts of the Latvian Provisional Government was to create a Ministry of Supply, whose purpose was to help cope with the prevailing shortages. It was endowed with the right to requisition, to take over food supplies and other products deemed necessary at a price fixed by authorities. This ministry set up workshops and small plants, which produced textiles, shoes, harnesses, soap, and other goods. The priority was to satisfy the needs of the army, with only what was left over going to the general public. The activities of the supply ministry were wide-ranging and included substantial purchasing abroad. Unfortunately, its activity was soon marred by corruption and other irregularities that kept prosecuting attorneys busy. The upshot was that the government abolished it in 1921. Parenthetically, after the peace came, the accumulation of useless goods in state warehouses took years to sell off.[3]

Other ministries were also engaged in similar allocation and supplying activities to meet the conditions of prevailing shortages. For example, in order to accelerate the revival of agriculture, the Farming Department of the Ministry of Agriculture tried to supply the farmers with agricultural tools and machinery, horses, dairy cattle, pigs, and sheep, though comparable services were already being rendered by the Ministry of Supply. As economic conditions improved by the mid-1920s and private enterprise took hold, the various ministries phased out their semicommercial activities.[4] A further reason that state-owned and state-run enterprises came into being was that Latvia, to a great extent, continued the familiar Russian institutional pattern. Having lived for so long under Russian rule, Latvians were used to the idea of the government's owning the railroads, operating the post office, and running the entire communications network, including phone and cable services. Therefore, almost at once after the declaration of independence Latvia turned over those branches of the economy to the Ministry of Communications. Only a small number of unimportant railroad spurs remained under private ownership. When radio broadcasting began, it became a state monopoly. Since the government owned and controlled virtually all railroads, it also took over and ran the repair shops for the rolling stock. Similarly, the Department of

Posts and Telegraph owned a workshop that produced telephones and, later, radios as well. This workshop eventually
became one of the bigger industrial enterprises in Latvia: VEF
—*the State Electrotechnical Factory.*[5]

There were a number of reasons for the next problem facing
the Latvian government—the great difficulty of generating sufficient income to cover all its budgetary needs. Although the war-
related expenses declined sharply after the war, the new government soon had heavy expenditures for the large and rapidly
growing number of government employees. At a meeting of the
Constitutional Assembly on December 16, 1920, one of its members, Roberts Bilmanis,[6] said, "The number of government
workers is close to 30,000 and it means that Latvia has one
government official per 50 inhabitants. . . . We have 46 departments, 9 different administration and superagencies, and 9 extra
directorates, so that Latvia at this time has a total of exactly 60
different departments. Such a large number did not exist in
either old Russia, the contemporary Soviet Union, or Germany."[7]
But the number of bureaucrats continued to grow. On May 1,
1921, the government's civil sector had 36,861 employees; by
January 1, 1922, only seven months later, the number was
38,437.[8]

Although to reduce expenditures, the government liquidated
some of its unprofitable enterprises, such as the Ministry of
Supply, that was not enough. For financing the remaining state-
run enterprises and for the creation of new ones, large amounts
of investment funds were necessary. Since the government was
unable to find alternative sources of investment funds, it got
them from the yearly budgetary allocations. In view of the postwar conditions, these were substantial sums for the newly formed
country. For instance, in 1927, out of the total budgetary
expenditures of about 160 million lats, one-fourth was used to
finance public investments.[9] During the first years of independence, collection of taxes was virtually impossible because
the per capita incomes were so low; nor did the central government initially have complete control of all Latvian territory. To
generate income, the government instituted high duties on both
imported and exported goods. However, the high duties, com-

bined with inadequately controlled borders, stimulated the growth of contraband. Because of these early growing-pains, before the tax-collection system was functioning properly, the government simply printed more and more paper currency to cover its expenditures. For instance, ". . . in the first few years of Latvian independence the emission of Treasury notes [paper currency] constituted the largest item of Revenue (82 percent in the fiscal year 1919-20, nearly 70 percent in 1920-21, and 22 percent in 1921-22)."[10] The result was a rapid, galloping inflation. Although the government managed to halt the continuously accelerating inflation by 1921, alternative sources of funds had to be sought to finance the budgetary deficits.

At first the government tried to borrow domestically, but the chaotic state of the domestic capital market, inflation, and the unwillingness of the populace to subscribe to government bonds made this an ineffective source of funds to meet current government operating expenses. For example, on March 18, 1920, the Latvian government decided to float a domestic bond issue at 4 percent in the amount of 50 million rubles (roughly one million lats), but eight years later only 50 percent of these bonds had been sold. It seemed that the people were aware that when prices rise in an inflationary spiral they should not buy government bonds.[11]

Similarly, to jump ahead for a moment, in 1931 the government floated a domestic bond issue in the amount of 12 million lats to finance the building of roads. The bondholders were not, however, entitled to the customary fixed interest. The government subdivided its total interest obligation to be paid into premiums and then distributed these to the bondholders on lottery basis. The total amount of these premiums, per annum, amounted to six percent of the amount of bonds outstanding. Yet, despite these incentives, this bond issue was so difficult to float that the government virtually forced these bonds upon government employees by deducting the necessary sums from their paychecks.[12]

The government also entered into numerous negotiations with foreign financiers for long-term loans, although without

much success because of the onerous terms, which usually
included concessions to exploit Latvian forests. Thus, except for
foreign debts made during the war of independence, when the
Latvian government bought weapons and food on credit, Latvian
foreign indebtedness was relatively small. The biggest foreign
debt incurred was $6 million from the Swedish match syndicate
Svenska Tandsticks A. B. in 1928. But even this loan involved
granting certain concessions having to do with the Latvian
match industry.[13]

The most effective way to augment government income
proved to be through the establishment of various state monopolies. As early as 1919 the government had set up a *FLAX
MONOPOLY*, which at first yielded large profits. Latvian farmers had been producing flax for a long time, processing it on the
farm and selling the flax fibre. After the monopoly was established, the peasants had to sell all their flax fibre to the agents of
the flax monopoly at a fixed price. This monopoly, in turn,
either sold the fibre to exporters or sent it to agents abroad for
sale. In 1919-20 the flax monopoly made a 751 percent profit on
the purchase price of flax; in 1920-21 it was 76 percent; and in
1921-22, 46 percent. These profits contributed substantially to
government revenues: in 1920/21 they represented 12 percent
of such revenue, in 1921-22 they accounted for 15 percent, and
in 1922-23 the figure was 8 percent. Because of the growers' dis-
content with the low fixed prices paid by the flax monopoly,
many of them reduced their acreage, while others sold flax fibre
to illegal buyers who offered better prices. These buyers in turn
transported the flax to Estonia, where no flax monopoly existed
and higher prices prevailed.

By April 1, 1927, the government's flax monopoly retained
only a certain portion of the earned profits, and returned the
rest to the farmers who had sold their flax to the state at fixed
prices. Yet, even though the monopoly had many enemies who
wanted it abolished because it was an unwieldy, bureaucratic
institution that could not get as good a price from foreign buyers
as could private firms, the flax monopoly persisted until the end
of Latvia's independence.[14]

Another lucrative state monopoly was that established over liquor in 1920. It permitted the production of alcohol by some select private distillers, who were then required to deliver their entire output to the state liquor monopoly. Consumers could buy spirits at fixed prices from specially licensed liquor dealers to whom the state paid a commission. In 1922/23 and 1923/1924 the profits of the state liquor monopoly amounted to 13 percent of the total government income, despite considerable competition from contraband liquor and, of course, from moonshiners.[15]

The creation of state-run and state-owned enterprises and monopolies was additionally facilitated by strong nationalist motives or tendencies. Before World War I Latvians had owned no more than 10 percent of all the industrial and commercial establishments, as measured in terms of either capital assets or trade volume. The remainder was controlled by non-Latvians,[16] mainly Germans, against whom Latvians had to fight bloody battles in order to gain independence. After cessation of hostilities, the lot of Latvian businessmen became even more difficult because many of them had lost their property during the war.

Despite positive and negative government operational controls, non-Latvian-run private businesses succeeded in setting-up several monopolistic market forms, mostly cartels and syndicates. German commercial establishments established numerous secret cartel agreements in order to maintain profitable prices and drive out competitors, mostly the Latvian businessmen.[17]

For these reasons the Latvians felt that they would be able to preserve their political independence only when they succeeded in gaining a controlling position, not just in politics but in the economic life of the country as well. Even though the government tried to support a few individual Latvian-owned firms during the first years of independence, their development was slow and not very successful. Nevertheless, in order to protect the Latvian economy from non-Latvians, in particular the German influence, the government tried to increase the number of state-run and state-owned enterprises in important sectors of the economy, to keep them controlled by the government bureaucracy and by the dominant ethnic group (see Table 1).

Table 1.

THE NATIONALITY COMPOSITION OF
THE POPULATION IN LATVIAN TERRITORY[18]

	1897		1920		1930		1935	
	Millions	%	Millions	%	Millions	%	Millions	%
	1.93	100	1.60	100	1.90	100	1.95	100
Latvians	1.32	68.3	1.16	72.8	1.39	73.4	1.47	75.5
Russians	0.23	12.0	0.12	7.8	0.20	10.6	0.21	10.6
Jews	0.14	7.4	0.08	5.0	0.09	5.0	0.09	4.8
Germans	0.12	6.2	0.06	3.6	0.07	3.7	0.06	3.2
Poles	0.07	3.4	0.05	3.4	0.06	3.1	0.05	2.5

The important point to keep in mind is that as late as 1935, one-quarter of the entire population consisted of minority groups, such as the Old-Believers of Lettgallia, who had settled there in the seventeenth century, Germans, Jews, and Poles. The German group, even though small in numbers, played an enormous role in Latvia in general, and in its economy in particular.[19]

Banks played a crucial role in the effort to increase state-owned enterprise. As early as 1921 the government operated its own bank, the State Savings and Commercial Bank. In 1922 the government restructured the bank by enlarging its capital and endowing it with the right to issue notes. Its name was changed to the Latvijas Banka (Latvian Bank). The bank served as the government's fiscal agent and holder of the government's funds. Since the government's budget, beginning in 1922-23, showed a considerable surplus, the Latvian Bank had large sums at its disposal for its purely commercial operations; it considered it a duty to compete with private banks, the largest of which belonged to foreigners.[20]

To provide farmers with the cheapest possible long-term credit, in 1922 the government set up the State Land Bank, buying up its bonds at face value with funds especially provided by the budget for this purpose. This was followed in 1924 by government sponsorship of the Latvian Mortgage Bank, which worked on similar principles to provide long-term loans where city-located real estate could serve as collateral. With the control of these banks the government held virtually a monopoly position in long-term credit. Ironically, however, because the government was still not in a position to provide both banks with sufficient funds, they in turn were limited in their ability to grant credit. Because Latvia had almost no bond or stock market, the bonds of the two banks were not traded on the capital market, with the result that there was no connection between money and capital markets. It was therefore much easier to obtain short-term credit than long-term credit. Many industrial and commercial enterprises had tied up a substantial portion of short-term credits in long-term investment, a practice which caused great difficulties and frequently threatened their very existence.[21]

Finally, during the first years of independence, the Social Democratic Workers' Party, the oldest political party in Latvia, exerted a strong influence on the Latvian economy. In the 1920 election of the Constitutional Assembly, this party obtained 38.7 percent of the total vote, making it the largest political party in the Assembly. In subsequent years, in the elections of the Latvian parliament, or *Saeima*, this party lost seats, even though it continued to get more votes than any other political party.[22] It was the social democrats who insisted on increasing state ownership of the national wealth, establishing the state monopolies, and controlling the actual running of government enterprises. When the Constitutional Assembly debated the proposed agrarian reform legislation (which will be discussed later), this political party defended the idea that all land to be expropriated should be retained by the government as state property and that landless peasants should not acquire land as property but only as a lifelong lease. The Constitutional Assembly eventually decided that peasants should be permitted to receive land in private ownership, but that those who so wished could opt to rent it for life. Significantly, when the Land reform was implemented *only one person* preferred the lifetime rental holding to outright ownership. Many of the social democrats themselves preferred land ownership.[23]

From December 19, 1926, to January 23, 1928, some Latvian

cabinet members were social democrats. During this period the social democrat finance minister created two more state monopolies: the sugar monopoly, which eventually owned three sugar-producing plants, and the grain monopoly.[24]

Needless to say, some corruption in the government enterprises and state monopolies caused considerable losses to the national treasury—losses that had to be borne by the taxpayers instead of by the owners of businesses, as happens under a private enterprise system. However, it is important to keep in mind that the prevailing spirit of the time had committed the government to the creation of more and more monopolies and state-owned and state-run businesses, thus force-drafting the public sector. Such practices hindered economic and structural change; they also produced real obstacles in the way of development of a strong private sector with flourishing private enterprise. Despite these handicaps and inherent problems, the trend towards establishing state-owned and state-run enterprises continued so rapidly that by 1930 the government owned one-third of the national wealth,[25] whereas at the moment of the proclamation of independence in 1918 the government had owned virtually nothing and its treasury had been empty.

NOTES

1. Latvijas Banka, *Activities of Latvijas Banka in 10 Years: 1922-1932* (Rīga: State Printing Office, 1933), p. 101.

2. J. Bokalders, "Finanču Ministrija," in *Latvija Desmit Gados* (Rīga, Jubilejas Komisijas Izdevums, 1928), p. 100.

3. *Ibid.*, p. 108; and A. Kārkliņš, *Mūsu naudas reforma* (Rīga, 1927), p. 226.

4. Kārkliņš, *op. cit.* p. 227.

5. Latvia, Valsts Statistiskā Pārvalde, *Latvijas Statistiskā Gada Grāmata 1929 Gads* (Rīga, 1930), p. 194; A. Rode, "Latvijas Dzelzceļu Politika," in *Latvijas Republika Desmit Pastāvēšanas Gados* (Rīga, 1928), p. 287; *ibid.*, pp. 306-307.

6. Not Dr. Alfred Bilmanis, the late Envoy Extraordinary and Minister Plenipotentiary of Latvia to the United States.

44 *Entrepreneur in a Small Country*

7. Latvia, *Latvijas Satversmes Sapulces Stenogrammas, 1920,*
session of December 16, 1920, p. 1703.

8. Kārklinš, *op. cit.,* p. 241.

9. Latvijas Banka, *Activities of Latvijas Banka in 10 Years:
1922-1932* (Rīga: State Printing Office, 1933), p. 65.

10. *Ibid.,* p. 53.

11. Bokalders, *op. cit.,* "Finančumirija" Ministrija," p. 106.

12. *Ekonomists* no. 20 (1934), pp. 705-708.

13. *Likumu un Ministru Kabineta Rīkojumu Krājums* no. 27
(1928), pp. 671-679.

14. Aizsilnieks, pp. 130-131, p. 213, and pp. 283-286.

15. Latvijas Banka, *op. cit.,* p. 62.

16. A. Klive, *Latviešu Pilsonības Saimnieciskā Politika: 1918-
1928* (Rīga, Paju sabiedribas "Zemnieku Domas" izdevums,
1928), p. 8.

17. *Ekonomists* nos. 13/14 (1937), p. 509.

18. *Latviešu Konversācijas Vārdnīca,* vol. 10 (Rīga: A. Gulb-
ja Apgādība, 1933-1934), pp. 20437-20440; see also J. Rutkis
(ed.), *Latvia Country and People* (Stockholm: Latvian National Foundation, 1967), p. 302. As late as 1935, one-fourth of Latvia's population were minorities, but economically only the Jews
and Germans played an enormous role.

19. J. v. Hehn, *Lettland zwischen Demokratie und Diktatur.
Zur Geschichte des Lettländischen Staatsstreichs vom 15. Mai
1934* (München: Isar Verlag, 1957), p. 6.

20. Latvijas Banka, *op. cit.,* pp. 9-14.

21. Aizsilnieks, pp. 326-335.

22. *Latviešu Konversācijas Vārdnīca,* vol. 11 (1934-1935),
p. 21001.

23. *Latvijas Agrārā Reforma* (Rīga: Zemkopības Ministrijas
Izdevums), 1930, pp. 194-195; and 1938, p. 456.

24. V. Bastjānis, *Demokratiskā Latvija* (Stockholm: E. Og-
rins, 1966), pp. 223-226.

25. *Ekonomists,* no. 5 (1935), p. 145.

V

Latvian Agriculture and Forestry: Some Unexpected Consequences of the Land Reform

To understand and evaluate the developments of Latvian agriculture and forestry some fifty years ago, it is useful to recall that economics deals with unique processes in historic time. Proper understanding of economic phenomena of any period calls for both a command of factual knowledge and an adequate sense of the spirit of the times. After all, economic ideas and economic policies originate from circumstances. The economist takes his cue from the politician, and any evaluations of human relations are bound by time and place. Yesterday's standards and values are inappropriate for judging today's economic policies and performance, and today's standards, even with the able assistance of hindsight, are inappropriate to judge the past.

At the time of independence, to reiterate an important fact, 48 percent of the entire land area of Latvia was owned by the big landowners and 10 percent belonged to the state. The masses of Latvian peasants were land-starved, and a speedy land reform was imperative for the young country. Between 1920 and 1922 the Latvian Constitutional Assembly not only wrote and adopted the constitution but passed the Land Reform Law as well.[1] Under this law all estate lands became state property and were transferred to the State Land Reserve. The former estate owners were allowed to retain only 125 acres each, plus or minus 10 percent. The state also expropriated those industrial enterprises attached to the estates which did manufacture products for local needs.[2]

The debates in the Constitutional Assembly about how to take over the estates were long and heated. Whereas the spokes-

45

men of the middle-class parties advocated compensation of the landlords, the Latvian social democrats wanted to have the estates expropriated without any compensation whatever. This thorny question remained unresolved until 1924, when the *Saeima* decided to pay no compensation for the landed estates that had been expropriated but to make the state responsible for paying their mortgage debts.[3] The decision provoked bitter resentment on the part of the Baltic landed gentry. They submitted a strong protest to the League of Nations, which rejected it after evaluating the explanation of the representative of the Latvian government.[4] Similar petitions by the German Balts of Estonia and by Polish landowners in Lithuania were rejected "on the ground that agrarian reform constituted a social, and not a minority, question."[5]

Of the many reasons that prompted the Latvian government to institute its drastic land reform, only the most decisive warrant examination. We have seen earlier how both the Germans and the Russians had made numerous attempts to colonize Latvia. All these schemes involved subdividing a portion of the estate lands into new farms for the incoming colonists. At the same time, many a landless Latvian peasant yearned in vain for "a corner of his own," because the landlords avoided selling land to them.

On March 1, 1919, while Latvia was occupied by the Red Army and was being governed for a short while by the Russian-appointed Communist government, a decree was issued concerning nationalization of the land. Its first paragraph stated that "all the land of Latvia (fields, meadows, waters, forests, and underground minerals) is being nationalized (expropriated) and is transferred to the ownership of the Latvian workers and its socialist Soviet government without any compensation to its former owners whatsoever."[6] All estates whose arable land exceeded 111.1 hectares (277.75 acres) were transformed into *Soviet* farms, i.e., state-owned estates with a paid labor force.[7] Smaller estates and all privately owned farms were left in the hands of the former cultivators, who were, however, now required to pay rent to the state for the use of land.[8] Many landless peasants had hoped that the Soviet regime would destroy the estates and give them land, but when it turned out that instead they had to work again on the Soviet-created and Communist-supervised estates as worker-peasants, they no longer remained sympathetic to the Communist regime. The leaders of the Latvian Communist party later realized that they had made a major mistake by not distributing at least a portion of the estate lands to landless peasants.[9] Consequently, the Latvian provisional government subdivided the state-owned large estates into small landholdings almost immediately upon the liberation of its territory from the Red Army, and thereby gained the loyalty of many Latvians who had formerly favored the Communists.[10]

Since the 'Baltic barons' had promised land in Courland to the volunteers recruited in Germany in 1919 to fight against the Latvian provisional government and the Latvian armed forces, the Latvian provisional government could do nothing less than promise land to its own Latvian soldiers. For this reason, one of the first steps of the Latvian provisional government was to decree that Latvian soldiers and their relatives would receive preferential treatment in the distribution of land.[11] A similar paragraph was also written into the Land Reform Law that was passed by the Constitutional Assembly.

After the end of hostilities in Latvia very few estate owners remained in the country. In the course of the war, the revolution, and the Communist rule, many landowners either had been shot or had left their estates unattended. The number of abandoned estates grew considerably after the Latvian War of Liberation, during which many big landowners had fought actively against the Latvian forces. Thus, in 1920 the state had to appoint administrators for roughly one-half of all estates that lacked landlords in order to raise enough food for the population.[12] The State Land Reserve consisted of 3.4 million hectares (about 8.4 million acres). Of these, 47.6 percent were actually distributed to landless peasants, the so-called new settlers, and others, whereas the remaining 52.4 percent of the entire State Land Reserve, which consisted mostly of forests, was left under state ownership.[13]

For the purposes of laying out new farms and other farm-related needs 1.6 million hectares (3.9 million acres) were used from the State Land Reserve. From these 1.6 million acres, 58.5 percent went to 54,000 new settlers. Of the newly established farms, 57.7 percent had 15 to 22 hectares (37.5 to 55.0 acres) and 23 percent had 10 to 15 hectares (25 to 37.5 acres), and 6 percent had less than 10 hectares (25 acres).[14] Another 20.2 percent of the land actually distributed went to 9,800 peasants who had formerly rented their land from the estate owners. Of these farms, 50 percent had 55 to 125 acres and 32 percent had less than 55 acres. Of the remaining land actually distributed, 9.1 percent was used for providing additions to very small already existing farms; 2.4 percent, for setting up social facilities; 1.2 percent, for the creation of artisan-farms, with an average size of 4.5 acres; and 0.6 percent, for about 1,500 orchards, truck farms and nurseries.[15] The remaining 8 percent was used for a variety of farm purposes. The land was not distributed *gratis*. All recipients of all land had to make certain "redemption payments" for it to the government authorities.

Most of the new farms went to Latvians because, except for some parts of Lettgallia, very few non-Latvians lived in the rural areas. It is important to stress that the various land reform laws had no discriminatory clauses against minorities in Latvia, exclusive of the supplement to the Land Reform Law of November 22, 1929, according to which preferential treatment in the allocation of land for the Latvian soldiers would not apply to those who in 1919 had served in German units that actively fought against the democratic government of Latvia.[16] The above data indicate that the Land Reform created a large number of small farms, probably in an effort to satisfy as many requests for land as possible, despite the assertion in the fall of 1929 that only 20,000 out of some 57,000 Latvian soldiers had received land as promised during the War of Liberation.[17] The distributed land, furthermore, was not always used for the purpose it was given. For instance, although the intent of the so-called artisan-farms was to facilitate settlement of artisans in the countryside, where they would be more accessible to farmers, most of this land was acquired by persons who were not artisans. Moreover, the allocation of land as a token of national gratitude

to former soldiers who had fought for Latvia's independence did
not foster the desired rapid growth of agriculture either, because,
as it turned out, many of these land recipients had no intention
of farming it. They simply sold their allotments as soon as they
got it.[18]

From a social point of view, on the other hand, the Land
Reform was a success,[19] insofar as it accomplished its purpose
of increasing the number of small Latvian farm holdings.[20] However, social and economic criteria for judging the success or
failure of the Land Reform are two different things. Very few
Latvian authors have broached this aspect of the Land Reform.
For instance, the late Professor Arnolds Spekke was highly
sceptical of Professor Herbert Heaton, who, in his *Economic History of Europe* (New York: Harper, 1936, p. 490), expressed the
feeling that the dividing up of the large landed properties would
result in a rapid fall of grain production.[21] And yet the evidence
of the Latvian grain imports in the 1920s bore out Heaton's pessi-
mism. Latvian sources are particularly revealing on the grain *ingo*,
a concept denoting the grain received by farms from outside, i.e.,
bought, and *outgo*, reflecting farm sales of grain produced by the
newly created farms. It follows from the 1929-30 agricultural output data, collected by the Latvian Statistical Administration, that
*the newly created farmsteads received 50 percent more grain than
they sold;* i.e., per year their grain *ingo* exceeded the grain *outgo*
by more than 50 percent. It was one of the unexpected paradoxes
of the Latvian Land Reform. Thus, the newly created small farms
became *net-users* instead of *net-producers* of grain; the very opposite result had been expected by the promulgators of the Land
Reform.[22] The urban population, which had hoped to benefit
from the redistribution of land by way of greater availability of
grain, was in actuality supplied by the old and established large
farms, supplemented by grain imports.

Generally speaking, Latvia imported considerable amounts
of grain in the 1920s. For instance, in 1927 more than 100,000
tons were brought in at the cost of 34 million lats in foreign
exchange.[23] The reasons for this situation deserve closer examination. First, the newly created *one-* or *two-horse farms* turned

out to be much too small to be efficient grain producers, because their relatively small arable land area did not lend itself to efficient utilization of agricultural machinery.

Another reason was the fact that the world grain prices, starting with 1921, showed a downward trend, whereas prices of the milk products, especially butter, rose. For instance, by 1927, rye prices had declined by some 30 percent whereas the price of butter had risen by some 50 percent. Under such circumstances, it was only natural that Latvian agriculture underwent rapid and significant structural changes. The favorable price trends for dairy products on the European markets led to rapid development of dairy farming and hog-breeding.[24] Already by 1925, the number of dairy cows had reached 915,800, a number exceeding the amount of cattle stock in 1913.[25] For this reason the Latvian exports of butter were able to increase rapidly; so that by 1929 they represented 21.5 percent of the total value of all goods exported.[26] At the same time, the export of linen fibres declined from 26 percent of the 1924 total value of merchandise exports to a mere 5 percent in 1929.[27]

In marked contrast to the rapid growth of dairy farming, the total acreage of rye and wheat cultivation grew very slowly. Not until 1933—after the Latvian government restricted grain imports and began paying high prices for the home-grown grain —did the rye and wheat acreage reach the 1908-1913 average of 957,000 acres, at which time imports of these commodities ceased. But a new problem arose then: what to do with the constantly growing grain stocks in government silos? Exportation would only have resulted in huge losses because grain prices throughout the 1930s were considerably lower than in Latvia. In fact, Ludvigs Ehkis, Latvian finance minister (1934-1938), stated that in the mid-1930s the government paid the farmers 100 percent more for their grain than the prevailing world prices.[28] This problem was never successfully resolved during the independence period.

Another unexpected result of the Land Reform was that small farms had much underutilized labor, whereas the larger farms, especially those that had existed prior to World War I, suffered from farm labor shortages. Since the disparities could not be resolved, Latvia was compelled to import a large number of farm workers from neighboring Poland and Lithuania. Thus, by 1929 Latvia employed 18,000 foreign farm workers, and, by 1931, the number had grown to 24,000.[29]

After Latvia became independent, the state took over ownership of all the forests that had belonged to the private estates, which went to the State Land Reserve for distribution, in accordance with the Land Reform Law. The agricultural census of 1923 ascertained that the state owned 1.5 million hectares (3.75 million acres) or 86 percent of all Latvian forests.[30] Thus, for all practical purposes, the government had a national forest monopoly, since what it did not own consisted only of small forested areas belonging primarily to those few peasants who had owned their farms before World War I. The principal reason for the state's retention of the forests was the belief that state ownership and management would be conducive to a more rational utilization of the country's timber resources than would be the case under private enterprise.[31] At the very beginning of Latvia's independence, a Forest Utilization Administration had been set up, but its activity was marred by huge losses, and it was therefore abolished in 1921.[32] The care of the forests was in the hands of the Forestry Department of the Ministry of Agriculture, which employed well-trained foresters and decided on the yearly cutting. Whereas the Forestry Department supervised almost exclusively the cultivation of forests, the actual utilization of forests was determined by the executive branch of the government. And since no one party remained in control of the government for too long, the ministry often changed its mind; the resulting instability often worked at cross purposes to the requirements of rational and orderly utilization of the forests.[33]

In the budget year 1923/24, the Forestry Department assumed responsibility for the cultivation as well as the utilization of its forests.[34] Although at first this activity was limited, it gradually expanded, until by the end of the fiscal year 1933-34 the Forestry Department had cut more timber on its own than it had sold forests for felling to independent buyers.[35] The government allocated substantial funds for working capital, for which the Forestry Department at first had to pay an interest rate of 7 percent a year, and later, after January 1, 1933, only 3 percent. Of the yearly profits earned, 40 percent was to be turned over to the government treasury, 40 percent was to be added to the working capital of the Forestry Department, and the remaining 20 percent was to be used for premiums to the employees of the Forestry Department. Thus, the yearly selection and valuation of the lots to be cut by the Forestry Department itself was always done with an eye on the expected premium at the end of the year. The idea was to cut the best and most valuable trees for disposal by the Forestry Department and sell the second-best timber to private buyers.[36]

In 1924, the government started selling lumbering rights in the state-owned forests to private buyers in yearly auctions. To attract as many buyers as possible, and, of course, to bid up the price, government officials divided the forests to be cut into small lots. This practice stymied the work of the large, privately operated sawmills, because it was difficult, if not impossible, to buy many forest lots next to each other. The fragmentation inhibited the use both of mass felling techniques and of mechanized log transport. As a rule, timber was cut in winter, and horse-drawn sleds transported the logs either to the closest railroad station or to the bank of a river, which would carry logs in rafts downstream after the thaw.[37] However, throughout the independence years, every year only 40 to 55 percent of all timber cut had actually been sold at market prices. The rest was either given away or sold at greatly reduced prices. New settlers could ask for and receive timber from state-owned forests, but they had to use it for the construction of farm buildings. Needless to say, some recipients of this cheap timber sold all or part of it illicitly for cash. Similar yearly allocations were made and trees cut for use by local administrative bodies, nonprofit organizations, dairy associations, for the construction of fishing boats, building of bridges and roads, the rebuilding of war-destroyed farm buildings, the erecting of telephone and telegraph poles, for churches, and for the construction of homes for country physicians.[38]

This extent of governmental generosity led to an enormous waste of the national timber resources. To the economists, the *law of substitution* was clearly operating. Since timber was much cheaper than other building materials, it was substituted for concrete and metals. The result of such practices led to considerable overcutting. A British consular report in 1929 noted that Latvian timber would be negatively affected in the future "as the provisions for afforestation, although on a larger scale than hitherto, do not keep pace with the present rate of felling."[39] What had become obvious to the observer was that because of the amount of timber being felled, the yearly growth rate produced would have to be increased in order to maintain a proper balance and reserve of this form of national wealth. The government's attempt to run the state-owned forests without an independent public corporation was a costly experiment, indeed.

During the 1920s, timber and lumber were Latvia's leading exports, accounting for one-third of the value of all merchandise exports. Although the value of timber and lumber exports dropped in 1930-31, by 1933 it had increased to 35 percent of Latvia's merchandise exports.[40] In addition, Latvia also exported paper and plywood, whose value rose slowly until, by 1929, it was 7 percent and, by 1933, 10 percent of all merchandise exports.[41] Hence, in 1933, Latvian forests provided 45 percent of the total value of merchandise exports. This percentage could have been considerably higher if Latvians had used timber and lumber more rationally, had substituted other domestically available building materials for lumber, and had automated the woodworking industry. Even so, by 1938, Latvian timber and lumber exports amounted to 1,421,204 cubic meters and accounted for 3.5 percent of the entire world export, as compared to the United States' share of 7.2 percent and Finland's of 12.4 percent.[42] In sum, the strong *statist* tendencies of the government prevented the rise of a strong and healthy privately financed and privately run timber and lumber industry. The economic consequences were counterproductive. Isn't a similar phenomenon evident today worldwide in the developing countries?

NOTES

1. The basic sources in Latvian are: *Latvijas Agrārā Reforma* (Rīga: Zemkopības Ministrija, 1930) and *Latvijas Agrārā Reforma* (Rīga: Zemkopības Ministrija, 1938). For some interpretative material in English, see W. v. Bülow, "Social Aspects of Agrarian Reform in Latvia," *International Labour Review*, vol. 20 (1929), pp. 38-43; and Royal Institute of International Affairs, *The Baltic States: A Survey of the Political and Economic Structure and the Foreign Relations of Estonia, Latvia, and Lithuania* (London: Oxford University Press, 1938), pp. 29-30.

2. *Latvijas agrārā reforma* (Rīga: Zemkopības ministrijas izdevums, 1930), p. 278 and *Supplement*, p. 1.

3. *Ibid., Supplement*, pp. 9-10.

4. *Materiāli Latvijas agrārās reformas vēsturei* (Rīga: K/s Latvju kultūra, 1929).

5. Royal Institute of International Affairs, *op. cit.*, p. 30.

6. A. Svikis, *Agrārais jautājums buržuāziskajā Latvijā, 1920-1934* (Rīga: Latvijas valsts izdevniecība, 1960), p. 33.

7. W. S. Hanchett, "The Communists and the Latvian Countryside, 1919-1949," in *Res Baltica*, p. 89.

8. *Obrazovanie sotsialisticheskoi Sovetskoi Respubliki Latvii i sotsialisticheskoye stroiteľstvo v 1919 godu; dokumnty i materialy* (Riga: Izdateľstvo Akademii nauk Latviiskoi SSR, 1959), pp. 380-381.

9. P. Allens, *Padomju varas ekonomiskās politikas pamati Latvijā 1919 gadā* (Rīga: 1960), p. 32.

10. *Latvijas agrārā reforma* (Rīga: Zemkopības ministrija, 1930), *Supplement*, pp. 58-59.

11. *Ibid.*

12. J. Bokalders, "Lettlands Agrarreform," in *Lettlands Ökonomist*, 1928, p. 80.

13. *Latvijas agrārā reforma* (Rīga: Zemkopības ministrija, 1938), p. 62.

14. *Latvijas agrārā reforma* (Rīga: Zemkopības ministrija, 1938), p. 66.

15. *Ibid.*, p. 68.

16. *Latvijas agrārā reforma* (Rīga: Zemkopības Ministrija, 1930), p. 195.

17. K. Balodis, *Runas: III Saeimas Sesijās* (November-December 1928 to November-December 1929) (Rīga: Armijas spiestuve, 1930), p. 88.

18. *Latvijas agrārā reforma* (Rīga: Zemkopības ministrija, 1938), pp. 428-429.

19. A. Bilmanis, *Baltic Essays* (Washington, D.C.: Latvian Legation, 1945), p. 51 and 62; see also J. A. Swettenham, *The Tragedy of the Baltic States* (London: Hollis and Carter, 1952), pp. 53-54.

20. H.-J., Seraphim, *Lettland und Estland* (Breslau: M. & H. Marcus, 1927), p. 287.

21. Paraphrased by A. Spekke, *Ibid.*, p. 364.

22. Aizsilnieks, p. 358.

23. Aizsilnieks, p. 357.

24. Latvijas Banka, *Report for 1927*, Riga, p. 61.

25. Valsts Statistiskā Pārvalde, *Piensaimnieku sabiedrības 1909-1929: Otrs izdevums* (Rīga: Valsts statistiskā pārvalde, 1930), p. 22.

26. *Ekonomists*, 1938, gads, no. 22, p. 1020.

27. Valsts statistiskā pārvalde, *Latvijas ārējā tirdzniecība un transits* (Rīga: Valsta statistiskā pārvalde, 1930), p. X, and pp. XXIV-XXVI.

28. Zinghaus, *op. cit.*, p. 139.

29. *Latvijas valsts kontroles revīzijas darbības pārskats par 1931-32, gadu*, Rīga, p. 44.

30. A. Teikmanis, "Mūsu meži un vinu izmantošana," *Latvijas republika desmit pastāvēšanas gados*, (Rīga, 1929), pp. 363-364.

31. *Materiāli Latvijas agrārās reformas vēsturei* (Rīga, 1929), pp. 327-328.

32. Latvijas satversmes sapulces *Stenogramas*, 1922, g. 19, maija sēde, p. 1489 and p. 1497.

33. A. Teikmanis, "Latvijas mežsaimniecības apdraudētais stāvoklis," in *Meža dzīve*, no. 45 (1929), pp. 1460-1468.

34. For a detailed analysis, see Aizsilnieks, pp. 364-371 and pp. 519-525.

35. *Ekonomists*, no. 19 (1934), p. 675.

36. *Valsts kontroles revīzijas darbības pārskats par 1930/31 gadu*, Rīga, p. 60.

37. *Ekonomists*, no. 6 (1932), p. 223.

38. Aizsilnieks, p. 522.

39. U.K. Department of Overseas Trade, *Economic and Industrial Conditions in Latvia, May, 1929* (London: HMSO, 1929), p. 14.

40. Aizsilnieks, p. 406 and p. 552.

41. Aizsilnieks, p. 552.

42. *Globus-Jahrbuch des Deutschen Verlages* (Berlin: Deutscher Verlag, 1942), p. 42.

VI

Latvian Industry: From War to War

It was not only Latvian agriculture that underwent drastic structural change in the 1920s. Independence brought with it very serious industrial problems as well. Two of these were of paramount significance. The first problem, "separation pains," resulted from the loss of Latvia's vast Russian markets. Faced with this loss, the Latvian government had to decide whether to restore the large-scale industrial pattern of the prewar period. Due to the unprecedented destruction of its prewar industrial potential, and with no assurance of accessibility to the markets of the new Soviet state, Latvia was forced to scale down its industrial pattern to a postwar structure of small-scale plants, catering primarily to domestic needs. During the long years of World War I, practically all of Latvia's large plant machinery had either been evacuated to Russia or destroyed. After the war, empty factory buildings and totally or partially destroyed plants scarred the streets and outskirts of Latvia's capital like the pox. The second problem was how to give ethnic Latvians a greater share in the country's trade and industry. After gaining independence, Latvians believed, perhaps innocently, that political independence and greater control over their country's economic life went hand in hand. (Some fifty years later, similar ironic reactions were realized in the emerging countries of the world.)

The peculiarities of official Latvian industrial statistics must be taken into account when examining how Latvian industry fared after the First World War. In Latvia, every established factory utilizing machinery (mechanical motive power), as well as every non-mechanical industrial establishment employing at least five paid workers, was counted, for statistical purposes, as an industrial enterprise. Nonmechanized manufacturers employing fewer than five paid workers were recorded as craft establishments.[1]

Despite these enormous problems, when peace came in 1920, a quick revival of industry got underway. Industry expanded throughout the 1920s and 1930s, in the face of a worldwide depression that saw a cutback of 15 percent in industrial employment by 1932, as Table 2 demonstrates.

Table 2.
POSTWAR LATVIAN INDUSTRIAL GROWTH[2]

Year	Number of Industrial Establishments	Number Employed
1923	2,032	44,100
1930	3,013	72,100
1932	3,523	61,600
1933	3,788	70,400
1938	5,977	117,200

The figures in Table 2 suggest that during the depression the operations of the remaining large firms were either reduced or completely stopped. At the same time, however, due to the introduction of very tight foreign exchange controls and other quantitative import restrictions in 1931, numerous small establishments, which formerly were considered crafts, expanded their operations by producing goods that were previously on the "forbidden" import list.[3] Thus did Latvian craft establishments increase the number of employees on their payrolls and become industrial firms.

Another highly revealing point of Table 2 is that by 1933 Latvian industry had weathered the worst of the great depression. In spite of this fact, some people maintained that Latvian President Ulmanis, who from 1934 to 1940 ruled the country alone, had to scrap the Latvian democratic system in 1934 in order to overcome recession and get the country moving again. Incredibly, this myth is still being perpetuated by Latvian immigrants to the West today.

Prior to the onset of the Great Depression, forestry products formed the most important branch of Latvia's industry. In 1929, it employed 20 percent of all industrial workers. Next came the food and spice industry, employing 17 percent, followed by metal-and machine-making with 16 percent. Finally, the textile industry employed 14 percent of the industrial labor force. The first two of these industries played a vital role in the country's foreign trade, providing lumber, timber and butter for export. However, by 1933, after Latvia emerged from the depths of the depression, it was in the food and spice industries that 20 percent of the industrial labor force earned their livelihood. This was followed by the textile industry, employing 18 percent, with the wood manufacturers and metal- and machine-making industries each claiming 15 percent. By 1938, however, the relative importance of different industries had again changed; the metal-working and machine-making industry had become the number-one employer, accounting for 17 percent of all industrially employed workers, followed by the food and spice industry with 16 percent, the textile with 15 percent, and forestry products with 14 percent.

The great majority of Latvian industrial firms were small establishments. For instance, in 1935 the average industrial firm employed only seventeen persons. The smallest were the cooperative societies, which consisted almost exclusively of dairy cooperatives employing, on the average, not more than six workers. Industrial firms owned by one person, legally known as individual proprietorships, averaged nine employees, whereas each industrial corporation employed some 140 people.[4] The reasons for the existence of such small industrial entities were the narrow domestic market, the prevailing cutthroat competition abroad, and the strong tendencies toward self-sufficiency throughout the world. Moreover, the lack of basic raw materials —especially of cheap sources of fuel, which had to be imported— prevented the rise of new large-scale export industries or the reestablishment of former ones.[5] Then, too, it was virtually impossible to set up import schedules for raw materials and half-fabricates on a regular basis because of the frequent arbitrary changes in the customs duties ordered by the government in order to control not only Latvian trade but also the balance of payments.[6]

Industrial activity was particularly hampered by the many government decrees designed to cope with the worldwide depression. On October 8, 1931, for example, the government introduced foreign exchange controls that included a state monopoly of all foreign exchange transactions, the rationing of foreign exchange, and the introduction of import quotas for merchandise, equipment, and raw materials.[7] From then on, the privilege of importing raw materials and machinery depended to a great extent on the whimsical good- or ill-will of the faceless bureaucrats in charge of foreign exchange and import quotas.

The establishment of large, efficient, and low-cost industrial enterprises was also prevented by the existence of numerous government monopolies of raw materials. Latvian forestry offers a particularly instructive and disillusioning example in that regard. The lumber and forest-products industry consisted of a large number of small sawmills that operated some 800 log-cutting saws. Management consultants, however, calculated that a mere 80 modern log-cutting saws would not only have been sufficient to handle all the available timber but also would have wasted less lumber. But the modern sawmills did not come into existence. To found modern sawmills, when the government owned almost all the available timber, would have been what at that time was called "commercial absurdity." Modern sawmills needed large woodlots to supply enough timber for continuous operation. But, because of the government's system of selling marketable forests in small woodlots at yearly auctions, the large, private wood manufacturers had practically no opportunity to buy contiguous lots that would enable them to cut trees and transport lumber economically.[8]

This, apparently, was also the reason that Latvia never managed to establish a modern cellulose plant. Latvia exported wood pulp for paper making even though it would have been more profitable to turn the available wood into cellulose for export. Moreover, part of the wood used for heating purposes could also have been turned into cellulose, and coal could have been imported to advantage with the foreign exchange so earned.[9]

In the tune-calling circles of Latvia, it had been emphasized that ethnic Latvians had to secure a dominant place for themselves in industry in order to gain economic independence. In point of fact, ethnic Latvians owned a considerable portion of the single-proprietorship industrial establishments, as shown in Table 3.

Table 3.

OWNERSHIP BY NATIONAL ELEMENTS OF LATVIA'S
SINGLE-PROPRIETORSHIP INDUSTRIAL FIRMS, 1935[10]

Number of paid workers	Number of Latvians	firms	Ownership by percentages Jews	Germans	Russians	Poles
5-9	1,202	58.2	23.8	12.0	3.1	0.8
20-99	285	57.9	25.6	11.2	2.1	0.7
100 and more	30	50.0	33.3	3.3	—	—

These figures indicate that in 1935, relatively speaking, a disproportionate number of one-man proprietorships in industry belonged to Latvia's Jews and Germans, for the former accounted only for 4.8 percent, and the latter, 3.2 percent of the total population. Although these individual proprietorships accounted for 78.1 percent of the total industrial establishments, they employed only 37.8 percent of all industrial workers. Latvia's largest industrial enterprises were corporations, which, in 1935, in number amounted to only 4.4 percent but which employed 35.2 percent of all industrial workers.[11]

Another revealing feature of Latvia's industrial corporations is the fact that the bulk of the shares outstanding belonged to foreigners, as shown by Table 4. Usually the balance of stock not owned by foreigners was held not by ethnic Latvians but by Latvia's Jews and Germans. And ethnic Latvians resented this very much. (Similarly, Africans today resent the fact that in most recently sovereign African countries nonnatives, be they European, Arab, or Indian, have a preponderant influence in African economies. This seems to explain the contemporary nationalizing legislation in Uganda, Zaire, Nigeria, Kenya, etc.)

Table 4.
PERCENTAGE OF TOTAL CAPITAL STOCK
FOREIGN OWNED, 1930[12]

87.4 percent in the chemical industry

67.7 percent in the textile industry

56.2 percent in the paper industry

54.4 percent in lumber and wood production

46.3 percent in the metal-working industry

It is evident from the above data that ethnic Latvians played only a minor role in the country's industry in the 1930s. One basic reason for such gross underrepresentation in industry was that few Latvians had either the necessary entrepreneurial skills and experience or the necessary investment funds. It should also be recalled that Latvia suffered from an inadequately developed long-term capital market, so that industrial firms were compelled to use short-term loans for long-term investment purposes. The practice of investing short-term funds in buildings, machinery, and improvements had particularly disastrous consequences when the Great Depression descended. The banks recalled their short-term loans, and these could not be refinanced. This illiquidity drove numerous Latvian businesses either into bankruptcy or to the brink of it.[13]

Industrial firms owned by Latvians were also hampered and at times made virtually unviable by monopolistic organizations run by Latvia's minorities. Latvia had no laws that could either prohibit or limit the scope of the operations of these market-controlling organizations. How powerful they were was demonstrated by the activity of the cartel of breweries owned by Latvia's Jews and Germans. This beer cartel even bankrupted two breweries that refused to join it.[14]

At the outset of the Great Depression, when the government introduced quotas on all imported goods, importers almost overnight became monopolists who did not hesitate to raise prices. To fight rising prices, the government set up, on August 25, 1932, a special office of Price Inspector.[15] In 1933, the newly appointed functionary decreed price cuts for beer. But the beer cartel responded with a lockout. It laid off brewery workers and stopped the delivery of beer. The government eventually yielded to such tactics by agreeing to lower the excise tax on beer, a concession that preserved the profit margin of the breweries even though the price was lowered.[16] If the government itself had difficulties in coping with the cartels, what could an individual firm expect? How could a new firm establish itself at all?

Finally, in order to form "economic bases" for themselves, certain larger political parties supported some Latvian-run business firms in order to assure a future flow of patronage for their political activities. The result was that different political parties tried not only to strengthen and protect their "economic bases," but also to destroy or at least weaken the "economic bases" of the others. This kind of in-fighting led to the destruction of some Latvian-owned businesses.[17]

For these and other reasons, Latvian-owned enterprises did not even succeed in securing for themselves a solid position, let alone a leading role, in Latvian industry. Thus the government, as described in chapters 4 and 7, strove to increase the number of "national" enterprises—by taking over privately-owned industrial firms with financial problems, by creating state monopolies, or simply by buying out particular firms. Whereas in 1929 government-owned industrial enterprises employed 9 percent of all industrial workers, by 1933 such employment had risen to 12 percent.[18] Government-owned enterprises played a leading role in the metal-and machine-building industries, which, in the 1920s, already employed roughly 40 percent of all workers.[19] The number of government-owned industrial firms proliferated after the coup d'état in 1934.

Latvia's textile industry came into being in the second half of the nineteenth century, when the Latvian and Estonian part of the Baltic region underwent rapid industrialization. It is, of course, true that men knew how to twist fibres into yarns and weave them into cloth long before they learned how to read and write. The methods of making cloth changed little throughout the centuries until about two hundred years ago. Then, in the mid-1750s new machinery was invented that made it possible to weave and spin at unheard-of speeds.

It was this rapid change in the textile industry that the Industrial Revolution was all about. In the second half of the nineteenth century the Industrial Revolution reached the Baltic coast, where, under the heavy protection of tariffs, textile industries were set up and prospered by selling their output to the rapidly growing vast Russian market.[20] By 1910 the Latvian area had 52 textile enterprises with 12,143 workers, and in 1913 Riga alone had 50 textile enterprises with 14,587 workers.[21] However, during the war, in 1915, the Russian government evacuated virtually all of the textile machinery and thus destroyed this fecund branch of industry.[22]

After the proclamation of independence, Latvia's textile industry picked up the pieces, so to speak, and it started to grow rapidly. This bears closer inspection. By 1923 Latvia already had 241 textile-producing enterprises, employing 4,700 workers.[23] By 1929, 253 firms had 10,100 workers on the payroll.[24] Some of this increase in employment, particularly in 1928 and 1929, was due primarily to large exports of textile goods to the Soviet Union within the framework of the 1927 trade agreement discussed in chapter 1. Up to the end of 1929, Latvia's textile industry supplied roughly one-third of the domestic textile requirements, whereas two-thirds came from abroad.[25] At that time the Latvian Bank explained this state of affairs by noting that the importation of textiles was "enhanced by the fact that foreign suppliers accommodate local buyers with longer credit than our manufacturers are able to grant. The result is that the consumer grows accustomed to foreign goods and pays no attention to inland products."[26]

The Great Depression hit Latvia's textile industry hard. A shorter work week, lower wages and salaries, and growing unemployment considerably reduced the purchasing power of the population, while the textile prices on the world market dropped dramatically. Dumping and cutthroat competition were the order of the day, with every firm throughout the world trying to increase its exports. Foreign textile producers were able to penetrate Latvia's markets, and cheap foreign-made goods caused huge losses to the largest Latvian textile manufacturers, especially those that had imported large amounts of raw materials (cotton and wool) at pre-Depression prices.[27]

Employment in the textile industry had already started to decline in 1930 and reached its nadir in 1931, when only 8,900 in 251 enterprises were on the payroll.[28] A number of large textile firms informed the government that they were compelled by depressed economic conditions to lay off workers.[29] In 1931 the government increased customs duties on textiles and introduced import quotas to protect the textile industry.[30] The result of these drastic steps was soon evident. The importation of textiles —which in 1930 had amounted to 52.4 million lats (roughly $10 million)—by 1931 was down to 29.1 million lats; by 1932, to 12.7 million lats; and, by 1933, to 12.2 million, or one-quarter of the 1930 level.[31] Of course, these lower values largely reflected the impact of the tight foreign exchange controls introduced in 1931 as well as lower textile prices prevailing abroad. However, in 1932 the activity of the Latvian textile industry started to revive. Employment rose to 9,500 in 277 enterprises.[32] This favorable trend continued until 1938, when 412 textile enterprises were employing 17,700 people.[33]

The textile industry was one of those branches of industry in which the ethnic Latvians had the smallest influence. For instance, in 1935 the gross value of the entire output of the textile industry came to 72 million lats, of which, 60.1 millions' worth was produced by the larger private limited companies or corporations, and of this sum 84 percent originated in German- or Jewish-owned firms.[34] The cotton industry developed into the principal branch of the Latvian textile industry. For example, in 1933 it employed 4,000 workers in 36 enterprises.[35] It grew at a brisk pace, so that by 1938 it had 41 enterprises with 6,100 workers, which accounted for 34.5 percent of the entire employment in the textile field.[36]

The Great Depression had hit the cotton industry hardest. To cope with the prevailing adverse economic conditions, the seven largest cotton-working firms had formed a syndicate in 1930, which was incorporated as Latvian Cotton Products (Latvijas kokvilnas ražojumi). This syndicate determined the output quotas for its members, marketed their output, and set prices as well. Only ten small weaving mills, which accounted for roughly one-fifth of the total employment of the existing syndicate, remained unorganized. But, because the syndicate controlled *all* the cotton-spinning mills, it could set prices at will for cotton yarn and thus keep outsiders in line.

The introduction of foreign exchange controls, high import duties on textiles, as well as import quotas for textiles in 1931, eliminated, for all practical purposes, all foreign competition for the Latvian cotton industry. Under this protective umbrella, the syndicated firms quickly made up their losses and kept on making substantial profits for a number of years thereafter. The authoritarian government of Ulmanis liquidated the syndicate in 1938, bought out one of the participating firms (Buffalo Corporation), and created a national, government-owned enterprise known as Latvian Cotton, Incorporated (Latvijas kokvilna).[37]

The second largest branch of the textile industry was wool production, which had led the field earlier when, in 1926, it consisted of some 147 enterprises with a total employment of 2,300 workers, or 34.8 percent of all persons employed in the textile field.[38] This branch prospered even throughout the depression years up to 1936, when 190 wool-working firms employed 5,300 workers, or 31.7 percent of the entire employment in the textile industry.[39] In that year, the wool-working industry was staggered by the devaluation of the Latvian currency. Many firms had bought substantial quantities of foreign wool on credit and, after the devaluation, had to repay their obligations in foreign currency at a considerably higher cost in terms of the lat.[40] In fact, devaluation aggravated these debts by some 60 percent. For this reason, after 1936 activity in the wool industry slowed down. But by 1938 the worst was over, and some 202 enterprises employed 5,200 workers, or 29.2 percent of all textile workers, thus earning the second-rank position in the textile field.[41] While the largest wool firms were located in Riga, over 100 wool-spinning and weaving mills in the provinces worked up the local wool supplied by farmers.[42]

During the Ulmanis regime, in 1937, the government bought

the entire stock of *Riga's Wool Manufacturers* (Rīgas vilnas manufaktura) and transformed it into the state-owned, national firm *Riga's Wool Producer, Inc.* (Rīgas vilnas rūpnieks), with a capital stock of 2 million lats.[43]

The third largest branch of the textile industry was the linen or flax industry, with activity centered in its spinning and weaving mills. In 1935, 2,800 workers were employed in ten major flax-working enterprises.[44] In 1938 nine such enterprises employed 3,100 workers, or 17.7 percent of all workers in the textile industry.[45] Whereas the cotton industry imported practically all of its raw materials and the wool industry not quite half its required supply, the flax industry used domestic raw materials exclusively. Whatever linen yarn was not used domestically went abroad and earned foreign exchange, while in Latvia the flax monopoly did all the buying and selling.

Last and newest of Latvia's textile industries was the rayon and silk branch. The first statistical data on it became available in the 1935 census, when nine silk- and rayon-working enterprises employed 1,500 workers.[46] Of these, *Rigas Audums* alone employed 1,100 people. This branch of textiles grew rapidly, and by 1938 it already employed 2,000 workers in nine establishments, or 11.7 percent of all textile workers.[47] The basic raw materials—natural silk and rayon—came from abroad, but the finished silk and rayon goods were destined strictly for Latvia's domestic market.

The foregoing statistical overview of Latvia's industrial progress reveals only the prelude to the emergence of successful private enterprises, such as *Rīgas Audums*, which firm shall become the particularized focus of this study because of the classical, case-book nature of its entrepreneurial activities.

NOTES

1. *Rūpniecības statistika* (Rīga: Valsts statistiskās pārvaldes izdevums, 1940), p. 2.

2. *Latvijas statistiskā gada grāmata 1926* (Rīga: Valsts statistiskās pārvaldes izdevums, 1927) p. 255; *1930*, p. 258; *1932*, p. 128; *1933*, p. 128; *1939*, pp. 133, 135.

3. Data on the industrial enterprises were collected every year, but data on the craft establishments became available only when the industrial and craft census were taken. For instance, in the 1935 census, Latvia was said to have 41,096 craft establishments employing 54,800 people; but later on it was learned that 86 percent of these were one-man operations. (See Valsts statistiskā pārvalde, *Mēneša biletēns*, nos. 1 and 2 (1937), p. 133.

4. *Latvijas statistiskā gada grāmata 1939* (Rīga: Valsts statistiskās pārvaldes izdevums, 1940), p. 140.

5. K. Kacēns, "Rūpniecības izejvielu apgādāšanas problēma, *Ekonomists*, no. 17 (1934), p. 585.

6. Aizsilnieks, p. 266.

7. *Ekonomists*, nos. 13 and 14 (1932), pp. 504-505.

8. *Ekonomists*, no. 6 (1932), p. 224.

9. Aizsilnieks, pp. 375-376.

10. V. Salnais and J. Baltais, *Latvijas amatniecība un rūpniecība 1935 gadā* (Rīga: Valsts statistiskās pārvaldes izdevums, 1938), p. 81°.

11. *Latvijas statistiskā gada grāmata 1939* (Rīga, 1940), p. 140.

12. *Latvijas statistiskā gada grāmata 1934* (Rīga, 1935), p. 186.

13. Aizsilnieks, p. 540.

14. Latvijas Kreditbanka, *Darbības pārskats par 1937, gadu*, pp. 189-194.

15. *Likumu un Ministru kabineta noteikumu krājums*, 1932. no 16, p. 235.

16. "Latvis," Rīgā, June 17, 1933, and Latvijas Kreditbanka, *Darbības pārskats par 1937, gadu* (Rīga, 1938), p. 198.

17. Aizsilnieks, pp. 272-274.

18. Valsts statistiskā pārvalde, *Mēneša biletēns*, no 11 (1934), pp. 692-694.

19. *Latvijas statistiskā gada grāmata 1929* (Rīga, 1930), p. 257.

20. Institut für Weltwirtschaft, *Die Textilindustrie in Estland und Lettland* (Kiel, 1939), p. 29 (typewritten).

21. R. Brenneisen, *Lettland: Das Werden und Wesen einer*

neuen Volkswirtschaft (Berlin: Volk und Reich Verlag, 1936), p. 342.

22. Institut für Weltwirtschaft, *op. cit.*, p. 30.

23. *Latvijas statistiskā gada grāmata 1926* (Rīga, 1927), p. 255.

24. *Latvijas statistiskā gada grāmata 1929* (Rīga, 1930), p. 233.

25. A. Zalts, "Tekstīlrūpniecības problēmas," *Ekonomists*, no. 5 (1931), p. 172 and p. 177.

26. Latvijas Banka, *Report for 1928* (Riga, 1929), p. 51.

27. Latvijas Banka, *Report for 1931* (Rīga, 1932), pp. 66-67.

28. *Latvijas statistiskā gada grāmata 1931* (Rīga, 1932), p. 218.

29. Speech of Finance Minister A. Petrevics on March 20, 1931 in the Latvian Parliament. See *Latvijas Republikas Saeimas Stenogramas VIII, III Saeimas sesijas 17, sēde*, p. 644.

30. Latvijas Banka, *Report for 1931* (Rīga, 1932), p. 67.

31. *Latvijas statistiskā gada grāmata 1934* (Rīga, 1935), p. 171. See also *Latvijas ārējā tirdzniecība un transzīts* (Rīga: Valsts statistiskās pārvaldes izdevums, 1935), p. XI and p. XVI.

32. *Latvijas statistiskā gada grāmata 1932* (Rīga: 1933), p. 128.

33. *Latvijas statistiskā gada grāmata 1939* (Rīga: 1940), p. 133 and p. 135.

34. Latvijas Kreditbanka, *Darbības pārskats par 1936, gadu* (Rīga: 1937), p. 105.

35. A. Elpers, "Tekstīlrūpniecības attīstība un stāvoklis pēdējos gados," in *Ekonomists*, no. 3 (1938), p. 120.

36. *Latvijas statistiskā gada grāmata 1939* (Rīga: 1940), p. 133 and p. 135.

37. A. Celminš, "Kokvilnas tirdziniecība un rūpniecība," *Ekonomists*, no. 3 (1938), pp. 128-30.

38. *Latvijas statistiskā gada grāmata 1926* (Rīga, 1927) p. 255.

39. *Latvijas statistiskā gada grāmata 1936* (Rīga, 1937), p. 146.

40. Elpers, *op. cit.*, p. 118.

41. *Latvijas statistiskā gada grāmata 1939* (Rīga, 1940), p. 133 and p. 135.

42. Latvijas Banka, *Report for 1928* (Rīga, 1929), p. 51.

43. Latvijas Kreditbanka, *Darbības pārskats par 1937, gadu* (Rīga, 1938), p. 29.

44. *Latvijas statistiskā gada grāmata 1935* (Rīga, 1936) p. 140.

45. *Latvijas statistiskā gada grāmata 1939* (Rīga, 1940), p. 133 and p. 135.

46. *Latvijas statistiskā gada grāmata 1935* (Rīga, 1936), p. 140.

47. *Latvijas statistiskā gada grāmata 1939* (Rīga, 1940), p. 133 and p. 135.

VII

Latvia Under One-Man Rule, 1934-1940

With the onset of the Great Depression a wave of one-man regimes swept Central and Eastern Europe in the newly created *cordon sanitaire* states adjoining the Soviet Union. Without much experience in parliamentary democracy and with new constitutions locating the center of power in the parliaments, a proliferation of multiparty systems had sprung up. As these led to widespread abuses, governments fell in rapid succession, and virtually all of them were eventually replaced by authoritarian regimes. In the early 1930s, the three Baltic countries had scrapped their former multiparty democracies and replaced them by what were then called governments of "national unity."

On May 15, 1934, Prime Minister Kārlis Ulmanis staged a successful coup d'état. He at once suspended all activities of political parties, dismissed the parliament (Saeima), and temporarily jailed many of the former legislators. Unlike Hitler or Mussolini, whose political base were the Nazi or Fascist parties, Ulmanis ruled without any political parties whatsoever. He ruled for years, uniquely, alone. All the emergency measures, the Latvian people were assured, were to be temporary and were designed merely to give the prime minister the necessary breathing space for action so that he could devote his entire attention to the more pressing political, economic and international problems.[1] This Latvian strong man paradoxically disliked the elimination of democratic regimes but felt that the existing excesses "of democratic representation rendered the whole mechanism inoperative."[2] He promised to begin work at once on constitutional reforms. That was Ulmanis's pledge; yet, at the time Latvia was incorporated into the Soviet Union in the summer of 1940, the country was still governed by that same one man, Ulmanis.

Even after some forty years, the story of Latvia's switch from parliamentary democracy to one-man rule is still marred by many irreconcilable myths, the most "sticky" of which is that there were too many political parties. This myth was invented, spread, and maintained by the opponents of the country's democratic regime and, depressingly, is still popular among Latvians living abroad. However, one recent book has set the record straight, so to speak, by noting

> that anyone who is familiar with the Latvian Constitution knows that the number of political parties had nothing to do with the Constitution. As a matter of fact, in Latvian legislation the election procedure was prescribed not by the Constitution, but by a *special* and *separate Saeima* (Parliamentary) *election law.* In order to reduce the number of parties in the Saeima, retaining only the largest and most important ones, it was necessary to change only a few clauses of the election law. One had to introduce or add a provision to the above election law that, any party, which, for instance, would not win three deputies, will get none. . . . In essence that's what the West German election law is all about.[3]

Such a change in the election law of the Saeima could have been brought about by a simple majority vote of the Latvian parliament, unlike proposed changes of the Latvian Constitution, which required a two-thirds majority vote. However, Ulmanis was against any change in the election law for a good reason.[4] His party was not the biggest, and to stay in power he had to "horse-trade" with the numerous representatives of small parties. Furthermore, under the prevailing democratic regime his chances of staying in power were dwindling. For instance, his Farmer's Union party (Zemnieku savienība) was not doing particularly well in the elections of 1931; whereas in the first Saeima it had seventeen deputies, in the last Saeima it had only fourteen.[5] Ulmanis's personal stock among the electorate was falling, as demonstrated by the 1931 elections, when he was defeated in Riga, Livland, and Lettgallia. In Courland his party won three deputies and Ulmanis was number-three man, the lowest man on the list. In Livland, Ulmanis's party won six deputies, of which Ulmanis was number four. Given this trend,

Ulmanis probably did not want to risk elections for the fifth Saeima, which were set for October 1934. To assure himself of power, which was not provided by Latvia's constitution, he simply staged a coup d'état on May 15, 1934.

It is, of course, true that Latvia's election law was very liberal. For instance, any five citizens could form a political party, and a mere one-hundred citizens of voting age could present a list of candidates for the Saeima. Immediately after Latvia gained her independence, numerous political parties had been created along narrow religious, class, nationality, and business interests, instead of national lines.[6] Thus, as early as 1920, elected representatives to the Latvian parliament came from twenty political parties, and by the fourth parliament (1931-1934) twenty-seven political parties were represented[7]; to be sure, many of these parties had only one or two representatives in the Saeima. This form of democracy—what might be called *partocracy*—was unwieldly because of the continuous shifting of political alliances, which made efficient government difficult.

In the "partocratic" atmosphere, frequent downfalls of government ensued; so much so that during the first ten years of Latvia's independence the country had thirteen different governments,[8] an average of one new government every nine months. It was a milieu in which political blackmail flourished and party-affiliated gamesmanship became a way of life. Since governments fell in quick succession, lower-echelon bureaucrats carried on the day-to-day business of running the country as best they could—a form of government that might almost be termed a bureaucratic oligarchy.

It is true that Latvia's economy was hit hard by the world-wide depression of the 1930s.[9] What is false, however, is that Ulmanis's coup d'état of 1934 was responsible for the recovery of the country's economy; this is one of the cherished myths of Ulmanites even today. Economic difficulties could not have been the reason for the coup; they were clearly of political nature.[10] The bottom of the depression was reached in 1932; by 1933 there was a definite upward trend in the economy, and certainly by 1934 the worst was over.[11]

Latvia's parliamentary democracy turned out to be unworkable in the sense that it would not guarantee Ulmanis's continuance as prime minister. Thus, after he had staged a successful coup d'état, Ulmanis started to look for a *third way* of organizing Latvia's economic, social, and political affairs; or, as the last Latvian ambassador to Italy, the late Arnolds Spekke, wrote in his memoirs, "a third way between the Russian Bolshevism and German Nazism; even to attempting semi-fascist methods of maintaining our state."[12] Thus political dictatorship replaced the former multiparty democracy, and the government "gradually tended to play a more and more important part in the economic system, until its activity in some respects can be described only as state capitalism.[13] Formally, the private ownership of the means of production was retained, and there was no introduction of the quantitative-output planning of the Soviet type. What took place was a thorough bureaucratization of the economy under a variety of pretexts.

One of the virtually unknown Latvian volumes of early 1930s was *From Collapse to Planned Economy: Problems of Latvia's Rejuvenation: The Future of Latvia,* by politician-diplomat Dr. Mikelis Valters. This book contains such strong similarities to what Ulmanis did during his rule that one might infer that Ulmanis had studied it as a text, although he never mentioned it.[14] A sampling of a few of Valter's ideas might be useful for the appreciation of subsequent developments in Latvia's economy. For one, Valters develops the theme that individual initiative should be subordinated to national considerations.[15] He then mentions that in contemporary Italy, with its corporate economic structure, the national government had extraordinary powers that combined and represented all the national strivings for independence and sovereignty, whether political, economic, or moral. He felt that the only way out of the world-wide agricultural crisis was by complete reorganization of agricultural policy; the individual farmer's decision-making should be subordinated to government control; the Latvian agriculture suffered or did not develop as it could because of a widespread lack of modern farm management.[16]

Valters went on to plead for the abandonment of what he called the oppression of "unfettered egotism and brutal economic sanctions" and for the introduction of "'co-operation of all citizens and the corporative structure of the economy." He rejected a free-trade policy for Latvia, for he believed the most-favored nation clause to be meaningless. He reasoned that a free trade policy meant for Latvia large-scale flight of capital, and thus, under the given depressed conditions, self-sufficiency might prove to be better than free trade. In a word, he concluded that the best interests of, and sociopolitical solutions for, Latvians had very little to do with capitalism.[17]

The empty pathos of liberalism needed to be replaced by cooperation of the entire nation, Dr. Valters wrote; and, more precisely, "national co-operation gradually has to replace the existing profit-type economy." Lastly, the politician-diplomat deplored the fact that the so-called Latvian intelligentsia had no ideals, took no initiative, and as a rule spent their time and lives in offices, banks, and political parties.[18]

Latvians, Valters argued, must get rid of narrow class interests and try to pay more attention to national interests,[19] which called for a different economic order. Since Latvians were not experienced entrepreneurs and businessmen, in no time at all foreigners and minority groups had won dominant influence in Latvia's economy. By now the state had to assume control, to direct its own economy, and to remove from the economy unsound or Latvian-hating elements, in order to make Latvia economically as well as politically Latvian.[20] Such reorganization of the Latvian economy along Latvian lines would necessarily call for the removal of many business elements. It was, in fact, a call for a thorough Latvianization of the economy.

This sampling of the basic ideas of Dr. Valter's work reflects the spirit of the times and the frantic search for solutions to the many depression-induced problems. It becomes clear that he had little faith either in multiparty democracy or capitalist economics, nor did he have any use for Soviet totalitarianism.

On the other hand, Fascist Italy, still in its infancy, was radiating a strange charm with its promise to inaugurate a happy reign of class collaboration by getting rid of the class struggle and dumping economic individualism as well.[21]

In the second half of the 1920s, the Italians had set up paral-

lel bodies of workers and employers for each trade and occupation for the purpose of making collective labor contracts and
spelling out wage rates and working hours.[22] The two groups, in
turn, were subordinated to the national interests, and strikes and
lockouts became regarded as punishable offenses.[23]

After 1926 the "para-State enterprises grew like mushrooms
in the rich soil of the corporate economy."[24] The Corporations
Act of February 5, 1934, set up twenty-two corporations, for the
purpose of enabling the state to intervene more directly in
economic life of the various firms.[25] These corporations represented vertically grouped categories of enterprises, such as
cotton goods producers, for the purpose of controlling them.
The Fascists claimed that their corporative system was "equally
far removed from individualism and from collectivism."[26]
Italian industry was also "ordered to form 'a common front' in
dealing with foreigners, to avoid 'ruinous competition,' and to
eliminate inefficient enterprises."[27] Fascists, aiming at political
independence, wanted to pursue an independent foreign policy
without a "corresponding capacity for economic self-sufficiency."[28] In short, to contemporary observers, Fascism was
aggressive nationalism, representing "some third way between
Marxism and liberalism."[29] According to one observer, Fascism
was decidedly anticapitalistic in economic matters and illiberal
in political matters.[30] Yet, noted another observer, "Fascism gets
things done, and Democracy doesn't."[31] In desperation, men
grab straws or chase phantoms in the hope of solving pressing
social, economic and political problems. After all, in the United
States, at that time, 25 percent of the labor force was idle with
no hope of employment.

As stressed above, after the May 15, 1934, coup d'état, the
Latvian government tried to cope with political and economic
affairs by completely revamping the country's image. But what
kind of *social order* resulted from the one-man rule of Ulmanis?
To call it fascistic rubs many people the wrong way. The term
monolithic authoritarianism seems inappropriate since Latvia
indulged in no bloodbaths, either of the Soviet or Nazi kind.
Surely, after some forty years, it may be possible to discuss this

question with neither personal animosity nor enthusiastic praise for everything the Ulmanis government did.

Broadly defined, a given social order includes all the *political, ideological, institutional,* and *economic* arrangements that govern a particular society. Another useful term to describe the totality of the existing political, ideological, institutional, legal, and cultural aspects of a specific society is "social space". What was the nature of the Latvian social order, or social space, of the Ulmanis regime from 1934 to 1940?

Having destroyed *all* political parties, Ulmanis swept away the entire democratic structure of the country. He introduced a highly centralized form of administration, along the I-am-the-boss line; it was one-man rule, authoritarianism, or simply dictatorship. Surely Ulmanis was no Stalin, Hitler, or Mussolini, but one-man rule is dictatorship nevertheless. Aristotle, in his *Politics,* described for all posterity the three salient features of tyrrany: (1) the dictator humbles his subjects, (2) he takes away their power, and (3) he sows distrust among them.[32] Ulmanis may have been a mild and benevolent dictator, but he practiced one-man rule all the same. He was the *Vadonis* of the Latvians, like Nazi Germany's *Führer* or Italy's *Duce.*

Ulmanis did not subscribe to any ideological race theory like that of the Nazis, nor to the Marxist-Leninist ideology. In terms of an ideology, nationalism, or more exactly the pretense of nationalism, could be said to be his driving force. He wanted to be a charismatic leader, the good boss, who would eventually see to it that Latvia was truly for the Latvians. Latvian Germans and Latvian Jews controlled Latvia's trade and industry, and Ulmanis and his men implied that they wanted to rectify this situation eventually.

All this nationalism was a pretense, however, a mask, a smokescreen behind which Ulmanis tried to acquire as many privately owned industrial firms and privately owned banks as possible, regardless of whether they were owned by Germans, Jews, or *ethnic Latvians.* Such government acquisitions were then dressed up as corporations.[33] Under this smokescreen of nationalism, the government role in the economy kept on growing by leaps and bounds, and it was hardly noticed by the public at large.[34] (See chapter 8 for the case of *Rīgas Audums,* a private firm owned by an ethnic Latvian, Roberts Hirss, which the government tried to turn into a state-owned "national" firm.[35]

Ulmanis's government did not abolish the institution of private or corporate property. Nor did his government introduce the Soviet-type central planning. What the Ulmanis government did was to revamp the entire economy along the *corporate* lines of Mussolini's Italy. The official line was, according to Finance Minister Ludvigs Ehkis, "to strengthen the Latvian element in the country and in the economy," particularly trade and industry, where Latvians were not well represented.[36]

Such a reorganization called for mandatory cartelization of all firms, centralized supervision of all trade and crafts, and the growth of state-owned and state-run industries. In other words, it meant that the market forces ceased to perform the coordinating function between amounts demanded and supplied, eliminating shortages or preventing surpluses. Controls were introduced over prices, wages and rents. Market forces were kept in check rather than completely eliminated. But in addition to coordination of supply and demand, every economy must see to it that goods are produced efficiently. That is, a given output must be produced with the smallest possible input of resources. This quest for efficiency was partially sacrificed to depression-induced considerations. With foreign trade substantially diminished, Latvians were at times forced to produce items at home, regardless of cost. In a nutshell, Ulmanis changed the economy in the direction of state capitalism, where bureaucracy controls all the major branches of the economy but some private activity remains intact.

The changes in the institutional arrangements were marked by growing centralization, with the leadership taking on an air of something mystical to be praised, almost adored, while the individual had to bow to the wishes of the state. The entire country's administration was centralized; all important officials were appointed by the respective ministries in Riga, with Ulmanis making the most important appointments himself. All administrative power emanated from the top and filtered down; all responsibility went from the bottom up. The entire press was subject to censorship, as were radio and theater. Yet, to reiterate, Latvia experienced no mass terror; although the most outspoken opponents of the regime were either jailed or exiled, none were executed. Life was not drab in Latvia, even though the praises of the *Vadonis* were sung everywhere.

Whatever the Latvian social order of the 1934-1940 period is dubbed, we know now from the memoirs of the Latvian ambassador in Italy in the 1930s that the entire Latvian Embassy was busy translating the statutes of the Fascist *cameras*, or chambers, which Ulmanis supposedly wanted to utilize in his future plans for building the new government of Latvia.[37]

In 1935, the government decided to set up a special financial institution as a substitute for a number of privately owned banks. Known as the *Latvijas Kreditbanka*, it came into being on April 9, 1935; it commenced operations on April 25, and its doors were open to the public on May 1 of the same year.[38] The government provided this bank with a joint-stock capital in the amount of 10 million lats.[39] Later on, this joint-stock capital was slowly increased up to 40 million lats.[40] From a purely legal point of view it was a conventional shareholder's bank, but in its nature and functions it differed enormously from the activities of a typical commercial bank.[41] First, *all* the shares were owned by the government. Second, all the questions that, according to the conventional statutes of corporation law, had to be decided by the board, in the case of Latvian Kreditbanka were decided by its manager who also discharged the functions of the statutory manager. The manager of the Latvian Kreditbanka was appointed by the cabinet on the recommendation of the finance minister. All questions that, (again) according to the statutes applicable to conventional commercial banks, had to be decided by the board or the general meeting of the stockholders, in the case of Latvijas Kreditbanka were decided by the minister of finance. Third, this bank was not subject to the scrutiny of the state comptroller (comparable to the American General Accounting Office).

The law that set up this banking institution stated that any bank in Latvia that the cabinet, on the recommendation of the

finance minister, declared to be in financial difficulties would be
automatically turned over to the *Latvijas Kreditbanka* for liquidation. This law did not provide for any possibility of appeal
or recourse to courts. The decisions of the finance minister were
final.

During its first years of operations, *Latvijas Kreditbanka*
took over seven privately owned banks, and three more went
into voluntary liquidation.[42] By 1940, Latvia had only three
stockholder-owned commercial banks: *Liepājas Banka*, where
the majority stockholder was one *German* bank; *Latviešu Akciju
Banka*, which was largely owned by an *English* bank; and the
Ziemeļu Banka, which to a great extent was owned by Latvia's
Jews. Strange as it may sound, the government-controlled *Latvijas Kreditbanka* had eliminated all privately owned banks where
ethnic Latvians were owners.[43] Was that the way "to strengthen
the Latvian element in the country"? In the place of the liquidated banks, the government set up two more state-owned
banks, which were almost exact copies of the *Latvijas Kreditbanka*. Needless to say, they were given the legal form of a
stockholder-owned corporation.

By October 3, 1935, the Cabinet had considerably expanded
the authority of the *Latvijas Kreditbanka*. The additions to the
original law stated that when national and/or security considerations warranted, the cabinet, on the basis of the finance minister's recommendation, could authorize the *Latvijas Kreditbanka*
to liquidate *all commercial and industrial firms* that were unable
to meet their financial obligations or had gone bankrupt, in the
same manner as it dealt with privately owned commercial
banks.[44] Nor was there any way to appeal the arbitrary valuation of these firms by the finance minister. The London *Economist* noted with tongue in cheek that "a State-owned bank, run
by a Finance Minister, under non-appellable decrees, can clearly
accomplish much."[45] "It is clear that a State Bank, working on
these lines, is a department for the execution of State policy,"
was the *Economist's* comment.[46]

On March 12, 1935, the government added to the existing
credit legislation by ruling that "if conditions in any financial
institution demand urgent intervention by the Finance Minister,

then the Finance Minister may dismiss the elected members of the Board, Advisory Board, Inspection and Liquidation Committee and replace them by persons of his choice without holding new elections." The dismissed had no right "to ask for any compensation on account of being fired."[47] The significance of this was that from then on the government could charge the *Latvijas Kreditbanka* with liquidating any privately owned industrial or commercial establishment. And these, it will be recalled, had no recourse to appeal, all government takeovers being final.

In the late fall of 1937, Andrejs Bērziņš, the director of the *Latvijas Kreditbanka*,[48] reported that his bank had not only rejuvenated and strengthened the country's banking system but also established state monopolies, wholly or in part, of heavy industry, building materials, electricity, tobacco, brewing, confectionery and textiles.

The London *Economist* gives perhaps the clearest analysis available:

The method used is to form limited companies financed by the State, with the intention of distributing part of the shares among private investors. The idea is not so much to found new enterprises as to take over already existing ones, including those working with foreign capital. This policy is doubly justified in official circles: first, it is asserted that it is in the Latvian national interest to suppress the overruling influence of the alien, i.e., of Jewish and German as well as other foreign capital in Latvian trade and industry; and, secondly, it is emphasized that the new undertakings which have been founded with State capital are able to safeguard common interests and not simply the interests of the individuals who founded them.[49]

Such a rationalization of the activities of the *Latvijas Kreditbanka* is an almost verbatim exposition of Dr. Mikelis Valter's ideas. Is this a mere coincidence?

One of the major instruments for the reorganization of Latvia's economic life was through the so-called system of *cameras,* or chambers, which was in effect a partial transplantation of the Italian corporativism to Latvia.[50] In rapid succession came the Chamber of Industry and Trade, set up on December 21, 1934;[51] the Chamber of Agriculture, which was established on March

29, 1935;[52] the Chamber of Handicrafts, which was created on
December 30, 1935; and then the Chamber of Labor, set up on
May 7, 1936.[53] Two more chambers, one for the professions and
the other for art and literature, were established on May 5,
1938.[54] It was reported some twenty years later that President
Ulmanis apparently gave up the idea of reforming Latvia's constitution on a basis of political representation in favor of a new
state apparatus based on corporativism.[55] Each chamber consisted of from 90 to 120 members, appointed by the respective
minister.[56]

The first chamber to commence operations, in February of
1935, was that of industry and trade. Its chairman and other
board members were appointed by the minister of trade and
commerce. It employed a staff of certified accountants who reported regularly to it on the financial conditions of the firms
in all branches of industry and trade. On December 8, 1938, the
cabinet promulgated a law creating special industry groups
within the Chamber of Industry and Trade. The primary purpose of these groups was "to throw out unneeded firms," i.e., to
force them out of business.[57] In its administrative structure the
chamber resembled, but was not identical to, the Nazi Economic
Chamber.[58]

The *Latvijas Kreditbanka,* together with the various chambers, were quite successful in reorganizing Latvia's economy. In
fact, they virtually transformed it into state capitalism. By January 1, 1939, *Latvijas Kreditbanka* had already taken over for
liquidation thirty-one commercial and industrial firms, quite a
few large ones among them.[59] A number of these firms, especially if partly foreign-owned, were at first bought out by the
Latvijas Kreditbanka and thereafter either liquidated or reor-
ganized and replaced.[60] As new state-owned enterprises, they
were called "national" firms, and all of them were given the
legal form of shareholder-owned corporations. The shares of
these national firms were held, for the most part, either by the
Latvijas Kreditbanka or by other government agencies. Only a
few of these national corporations were permitted to sell their
stock to the general public, and even then no more than 25
percent of the stock outstanding.[61] By mid-March of 1939,

thirty-eight such national enterprises were in existence, in which either the entire capital stock or a substantial portion of all shares were government-owned.[62] Among the numerous national firms were: *Aldaris* (breweries), *Ādu un Vilnas Centrāle* (hides and wool), *Bekona Eksports* (meat and bacon), *Degviela* (fuel), *Drošiba* (insurance), *Dzirnavnieks* (flour mills), *Kalkis* (lime), *Kiegelis* (brick), *Kūdra* (turf), *Laima* (chocolates), *Latvijas Centrālais Sēklu Eksports* (seeds), *Latvijas Koks* (lumber), *Latvijas Kokvilna* (cotton), *Maiznieks* (bakeries), *Ogle* (coal), *Rīgas Vilnas Rūpnieks* (wool), *Šifers* (shingles), and *Vairogs* (auto assembly).[63]

With the establishment of all these state and seminational firms, a situation of tightly held and closely interlocked capital arose. This made the government's economic influence so dominant that no privately owned firm—including any financed by foreign capital—ever felt secure about its future.[64]

On July 9, 1936, the cabinet promulgated a law governing the industrial and craft establishments, stating that all firms were required to have a permit from the Ministry of Finance for future operations, and that the managers had to be Latvian citizens and to know Latvian.[65] If a firm wanted to expand, or change its production methods, or alter the floor layout of the plant—in short, anything that called for the installation of new or extra sources of power, or the addition of new machinery, or the recruitment of extra manpower—it needed permission from the appropriate government agency.[66]

Furthermore, in 1938, to compel the industrial firms to rationalize their production methods, the cabinet set up a special Productivity Institute as part of the administrative structure of the Finance Ministry. The institute's mission was to assess and recommend methods for improvement in the utilization of time and labor, mechanization of the production process, and standardization of products. At the same time, the minister of finance was vested with additional authority to issue binding decrees and regulations on rationalization and standardization for Latvian industry. He also had the right to punish violators of the reform regulations with fines up to Ls 2,000 ($500), or by simply closing the firm if violations persisted.[67]

But the hoped-for rationalization and mechanization did not materialize for a number of reasons. For one, Latvia at the time was a country of cheap manpower, as compared with the United States, for instance.[68] On the other hand, the cost of imported machinery and equipment was high, relatively speaking. Hence, by the law of substitution, Latvian industrialists used labor-intensive methods to produce goods and services. That is, they substituted the cheaper for the dearer factors of production. In Latvia it did not pay to utilize the capital-intensive mode of production. Next, Latvia's domestic market was much too small for mass-production methods of industrial commodities; with most European countries practicing self-sufficiency, or something resembling it, there would have been no way of selling abroad any output of Latvian mass production. And lastly, high import duties and other quantitative import restrictions protected Latvia's low-mechanized high-cost producers from foreign competition. Under such cozy circumstances, the exhortations of government bureaucrats fell, for the most part, on deaf ears.

On May 2, 1939, the cabinet promulgated a law governing job creation and allocation of manpower. Charged with its implementation was the Latvian Labor Office, still to be established, with its executive officer directly subordinate to the prime minister. The Labor Office had the exclusive right to allocate manpower. From then on, employees, except for persons above the age of 65, could be hired only with the permission of or referral by the Labor Office.[69] This law was designed basically to stop the massive *Landflucht* from the country to city, but in fact it merely provided another instrument of control over the private sector.

Furthermore, as early as December 13, 1934, the cabinet had passed a law creating the office of Price Inspector, with very substantial authority. From then on, nobody could increase prices either in industry or trade without his approval.[70] These examples of economic *dirigisme* were evident not only in industry but also in such other sectors as agriculture and trade.

The new administrative economic structure, which was created at a rapid pace after the establishment of Ulmanis's one-man rule in 1934, was most succinctly characterized by Ulmanis himself in a speech before the Chamber of Latvian Agriculture on February 4, 1937, in which, among other things, he declared:

> What, How and Who will produce is decided by political authorities, which have won freedom of action. When politicians in authority decide on questions of economic policy and dictate what the economy shall do, nobody should dare to meddle![71]

It follows, then, that if the government is bent on multiplying the nationalized enterprises and on deciding questions of "what, how, and who will produce," flourishing private enterprise is obviously well-nigh impossible, although nominally private firms may exist.

The results of the new economic policy may be seen in Table 5, which charts the development of net output of Latvian industry during the Ulmanis regime.

Table 5.
NET OUTPUT OF LATVIAN INDUSTRY, 1934-1938[72]

	1934	1935	1936	1937	1938
The value of net output in current prices (lats, millions)	196.3	205.6	217.8	269.1	294.1
The same in terms of 1934 purchasing power*	196.3	196.2	198.7	197.7	216.1
The average value of net output, per person, employed in industry, in thousands of lats	2.3	2.1	2.0	1.8	1.8

---

*The value of net industrial output in terms of constant 1934 purchasing power was obtained by dividing the value of net industrial output, stated in current prices, by wholesale price indices.

The figures in Table 5 demonstrate that the average value of the Latvian industrial output, per person, declined during the years

of the Ulmanis regime, although these were supposed to have
been the "good years."[73] One of the principal reasons for this
unfavorable trend was precisely the rapid establishment of national enterprises, which was accompanied by capital flight,
mostly of the illegal kind. This exodus of capital funds abroad
made the country worse off, because bureaucratic whim or
command never seems to be an adequate substitute for entrepreneurial talent, something that the hands guiding development
then did not, as they now do not, seem to grasp.

NOTES

1. J. Rogainis, "The Emergence of an Authoritarian Regime
in Latvia, 1932-1934," in *Lituanus*, vol. 17, no. 3 (1971), p. 78.

2. *Select Committee on Communist Aggression Report*, p.
116.

3. V. Bastjānis, *Gala sākums* (Lidingö, Sweden: Memento,
1964), p. 22.

4. *Ibid.*, p. 23

5. *Latvju enciklopēdija*, edited by A. Švābe (Stockholm:
Apgāds Trīs Zvaigznes, 1953-1955), p. 1988.

6. Rogainis, *op. cit.*, p. 62.

7. *Latvju enciklopēdija*, p. 1987.

8. Jubilejas Komisijas Izdevums, *Latvija Desmit Gados.
Latvijas Valsts Nodibināšana und Vinas Pirmo 10 Gadu Darbības
Vēsture* (Rīga: Valsts Tipografija, 1928), pp. 37-40.

9. Royal Institute of International Affairs. *The Baltic States:
A Survey of the Political and Economic Structure and the Foreign Relations of Estonia, Latvia, and Lithuania* (London: Oxford University Press, 1938), p. 143.

10. Aizsilnieks, p. 600.

11. *Ibid.*, p. 582 and p. 750.

12. A. Spekke, *Atminu brīži* (Stockholm: Zelta Ābele, 1967),
p. 291.

13. Royal Institute of International Affairs, *op. cit.*, p. 144.

14. *No sabrukuma uz plānveidotu saimniecību: Latvijas at-
jaunošanas problēmas, Latvijas nākotne*, Rīga, 1933.

15. *Ibid.*, p. 24.

16. *Ibid.*, pp. 55, 103, 111.

17. *Ibid.*, pp. 123, 156, 362, 369.

18. *Ibid.*, pp. 374, 375, 380.

19. *Ibid.*, p. 381.

20. *Ibid.*, pp. 383 and 385.

21. C. I. Schmidt, *The Corporate State in Action: Italy Under Fascism* (New York: Oxford University Press, 1939), p. 62.

22. V. M. Dean, "The Economic Situation in Italy: The Corporative System," in *Foreign Policy Reports*, vol. 10, no. 23 (1935), pp. 298-302.

23. A. Anselmi, "Trade Associations and Corporations in Italy after the Recent Reforms," in *International Labour Review*, vol. 31 (1935), p. 7.

24. A. Lyttlelton, *The Seizure of Power: Fascism in Italy, 1919-1929* (New York: Charles Scribner's Sons, 1973) p. 358.

25. C. Arena, "The Development of the Law Governing Employment and the Undertaking in Italy," *International Labour Review*, vol. 32 (1935), p. 171.

26. *Ibid.*, p. 175.

27. Lyttelton, *op. cit.*, p. 359.

28. Schmidt, *op. cit.*, p. 141.

29. M. Einaudi, "Fascism," in *International Encyclopedia of the Social Sciences*, vol. 5 (New York: The Macmillan Company and The Free Press, 1968), p. 335.

30. W. Röpke, "Fascist Economics," in *Economica*, vol. 2 (1935), p. 86.

31. F. Yeats-Brown, "Alternatives to Democracy: The Corporate State," *The Spectator, vol.* 151 (1933), p. 471.

32. Aristotle, *Politics*, Jowett translation, Book V, c. II (London, 1923), pp. 225-8.

33. Aizsilnieks, pp. 631-634.

34. *Ibid.*, pp. 606-610.

35. R. Hiršs, *Rigas Audums* (Stockholm: Daugava, 1965), pp. 104-111.

36. Zinghaus, *op. cit.*, p. 141.

37. Spekke, *op. cit.*, p. 243.

38. Latvijas Kreditbanka, *Darbibas pārskats par 1935. gadu* (Rīga, 1936), pp. 10-11.

88 *Entrepreneur in a Small Country*

39. *Pirmais gads, 1934. 15. V—1935. 15.* V (Rīga, Letas izde-vums), p. 100.

40. *Trešais gads, 1936. 15. V—1937. 15.* V (Rīga, Letas izde-vums), p. 107.

41. Latvijas Kreditbanka, *Darbības pārskats par 1937. gadu* (Rīga, 1938), p. 5.

42. *Ekonomists,* 1936, no. 5, pp. 185-186.

43. Aizsilnieks, p. 634.

44. Latvijas Kreditbanka, *Darbības pāsrkats par 1936. gadu* (Rīga, 1937), p. 12.

45. "Banking in Latvia," *The Economist,* vol. 122 (1936), p. 591.

46. *Ibid.*

47. *Likumu un Ministru kabineta noteikumu krājums* (Rīga, April 5, 1935), no. 6, p. 62.

48. Z. Unams (ed.), *Es vinu pazīstu* (Rīga: Biografiskā ar-chīva apgāds, 1939), p. 69.

49. "Latvia: The State of Banking, Trade and Industry," *The Economist,* vol. 129 (1937), p. 311.

50. Aizsilnieks, p. 611.

51. *Likumu un Ministru kabineta noteikumu krājums,* no. 19, December 31, 1934, p. 312.

52. *Pirmais gads. 1934. 15. V—1935. 15.* V (Rīga: Letas izde-vums, 1935), p. 92.

53. *Trešais gads. 1936. 15. V—1937. 15.* V (Rīga, Letas izde-vums), p. 26.

54. "Kameru sistēma," in *Latvju enciklopēdija,* edited by A. Švābe (Stockholm: Trīs Zvaigznes, vol. 1, 1950-51), p. 949.

55. *Ibid.,* p. 949.

56. Aizsilnieks, pp. 612-613.

57. *Piektais gads, 1938. 15. V—1939. 15. V.,* pp. 313-314.

58. The Nazi system had national groups, (Reichsgruppen), for each industry, such as trade, banking, insurance, power, tourist trade, and crafts. On the middle level of authority came the economic groups (Wirtschaftsgruppen), and at the lowest level of authority were the trade groups (Fachgruppen). For some details, see N. Balabkins, *Germany Under Direct Controls:*

Economic Aspects of Industrial Disarmament, 1945-1948 (New Brunswick, N.J.: Rutgers University Press, 1964), p. 48.

59. *Ekonomists,* 1939, no. 22, p. 1563.

60. Latvijas Kreditbanka, *Darbības pārskats par 1937. gadu,* p. 116.

61. *Ekonomists,* 1939, no. 3, p. 148.

62. Latvijas Kreditbanka, *Darbības pārskats par 1938. gadu,* p. 77.

63. Aizsilnieks, p. 653; and V. Bastjānis, *Gala sākums* (Lidingö: Memento, 1964), pp. 126-127.

64. "Latvia. An Authoritarian Economy," *The Economist,* vol. 134 (1939), p. 503.

65. *Trešais gads. 1936. 15. V.–1937. 15. V* (Rīga, Letas izdevums), pp. 51-52.

66. A. Zalts, *Centieni un sasniegumi nacionālā saimniecībā, Latvija 20 gados* (Rīga, 1938), p. 158.

67. *Piektais gads. 1938. 15. V.–1939. 15. V.* (Rīga, Letas izdevums), pp. 76-77.

68. *Ekonomists,* 1937, no. 23, p. 964.

69. Piektais gads, *op. cit.,* pp. 120-126.

70. Pirmais gads, *op. cit.,* p. 72.

71. Latvijas lauksaimniecības kamera, *Darbības pārskats par 1936-37 gadu* (Jelgava, 1937), pp. 28-30.

72. Aizsilnieks, p. 757.

73. A. Bērzinš, *Labie gadi* (New York: Grāmatu draugs, 1963), pp. 186-254.

Part II
Entrepreneurship

VIII

The Fruit of Innovation: Rigas Audums

Why was it necessary to write seven introductory chapters leading to the discussion of *Rīgas Audums?* The question is proper; the answer is quite simple. No enterprise or firm operates in a vacuum; it exists only within a given social order, which in turn affects its work crucially and leads to the development of other entrepreneurs. Thus, the need for the preliminary study of Latvia's economic, political, and institutional framework is self-evident.[1] *Rīgas Audums* began in Latvia, hence its operations are a part of that country's history, and vice versa.

The emergence in Latvia, within a short time and in the predominating anti-private-enterprise atmosphere, of a large and highly successful, privately owned textile company, offers a classic case history of entrepreneurship and government bureaucracy in conflict.

Established in 1925 in Riga, *Rīgas Audums* (Riga Textiles), was launched on the wave of the feverish postwar boom, even though Latvia was experiencing a slight slackening of economic activity and falling wholesale prices, conditions that were noticeable throughout Europe. The first bankruptcies occurred in Latvia in 1925.[2] It was not the most auspicious time for the establishment of a new business venture.

Nevertheless, *Rīgas Audums* set up operations in a rented cellar in Riga. At first, the factory's equipment consisted of three secondhand weaving looms in bad condition. The new owner-entrepreneur, Roberts Hirss, not only repaired the looms but also modified them himself. In addition to himself and his wife, Alma, who took an active part in the business from the outset,[3] his labor force consisted of *one* paid worker.

Rīgas Audums was a success from its first day. After two years of bursting at the seams, it had to relocate in a new building with new facilities and much more floorspace. By this time the company had 200 employees on its payroll.[4]

Latvia did not escape the effects of the deep depression that was paralyzing the entire capitalist world. By 1931, many of the country's industrial firms had been forced to cut back on production or close out operations altogether. But *Rīgas Audums*, an oasis in a desert, almost miraculously kept on expanding, until by 1932 it employed more than 500 people.[5]

To provide the necessary floorspace for expansion, Hirss bought a large industrial property that had been abandoned during the war. By 1933 he had renovated the facility enough to allow *Rīgas Audums* to move in.[6] The firm's employment rate continued to grow even more rapidly. By 1934, the number employed was 1,125; and by 1938, 1,600.[7] In 1939, the cumulative records show the sale of more than 2 million meters of various kinds of cloth and nearly 80,000 meters of batting.[8] *Rīgas Audums* had grown to be one of Latvia's biggest industrial firms and, undoubtedly, would have continued to expand were it not for World War II and had Latvia not been incorporated into the Soviet Union.

The proprietor and manager of *Rīgas Audums*, Roberts Hirss (1895-1972), was born in a small rural district of Vējava, Latvia, of Lutheran parents.[9] A farm boy whose formal education ended after only three years of elementary school, he worked as a shepherd or field hand. But his actual lifelong schooling began when he became an apprentice, at first in the local blacksmith shop and later in the local gristmill. At that time, Latvian water-run mills were quite small but highly versatile. They ground grain and made grits; they carded, spun wool, and wove cloth. They also sawed logs into building materials.

As an eager mill apprentice, Hirss became thoroughly acquainted with the various steps of operating and servicing the mechanical equipment. He quickly learned why some machines did not work properly, and how to fix them. His apprenticeship also taught him basic marketing skills at the local farmer's fair level, where he learned how to behave towards a customer and how to display and sell products. But he had other talents, too.

It so happened that at a mill where he was working, modern wool-processing equipment, manufactured by Oscar Schimmel in Chemnitz, Germany, was being installed. The installation and the operation of this machinery proved to be fateful, so to speak, for Roberts Hirss's future.

A big Russian landowner by the name of Petrov, a trained engineer, had planned to set up a modern wool-processing plant in his native country. His interest in the latest developments in the textile industry had led him to Germany and to Chemnitz. While there, the manufacturers of this new machinery suggested to him that he visit the mills in Livland and see for himself how such machinery functioned. One day he arrived at the mills and spent the next two weeks observing how the machinery worked. He was pleased with it and ordered identical equipment from Chemnitz. However, soon after the machinery arrived in Russia, World War I broke out and Petrov could not get the German mechanics to set it up. When the Russian landlord recalled the mill he had visited in Latvia, he invited Hirss and a few of his colleagues to come to Russia to set up the new equipment and work for him. The pay and working conditions that he offered were so tempting that Hirss went to live in Russia.

They installed the machinery, but wartime shortages were already asserting themselves in the form of shortages of raw materials and industrial supplies. In such circumstances, Roberts was sent to the Baltic provinces to buy up whatever needed raw materials and industrial supplies were still available. On his return, after a fortnight's absence, he learned that Petrov, who had a heart ailment, had died suddenly. His heirs auctioned the the factory, and Hirss had to look for another job.

With World War I in full swing, Russian textile plants were busy making cloth for the army, but the quality of output deteriorated continuously. At times as much as 40 percent of the output was rejected by the inspecting commissions, and firms could not deliver the contracted goods on time and had to pay heavy penalties. Instead of making expected high and quick profits, numerous textile firms were even losing money. Hirss's employer, however (at that time the Zoltov textile plant), was doing well and only 3 percent of its output was rejected by the quartermaster's inspectors. Such a performance was noticed by other textile firms, and soon Roberts Hirss was lured away by a large textile giant of Russia, the Asejew company. He was to become a successful troubleshooter, and his first assignment was to work in the plant with most quality problems. With patience and a systematic approach, he was able to streamline the operations, so that not only was the output of this division quadrupled but also its quality was raised. Afterwards he was assigned to improve operations in other divisions and later was made responsible for the continuous and smooth operation of technical equipment in ten plants employing some 35,000 workers.[10]

His experience in Russia served as Hirss's schooling in the textile field. Without teachers, he had to teach himself how to reach the core of a problem and solve it. Thereby he acquired the kind of skill and education that neither college nor any other institution could provide. In his spare time, he also obtained the equivalent of a Russian high school diploma through correspondence courses.

After almost losing his life in the Russian Revolution, Hirss returned empty-handed to his native Latvia in 1920, to start anew. First he had to discharge his military service obligation. Once this was behind him, he went to work in a textile firm in Riga, beginning as a common laborer. He took successive jobs in several firms to find out what the textile industry was facing in newly independent Latvia.

In 1923 Roberts Hirss married Alma Tinte. Born in Courland, she was the daughter of a farmer from the small rural district of Nīgrande. Alma had always been an independent child. For example, it was customary for everyone to kiss the Lutheran minister's hand after church services. Alma refused. Her parents were ashamed of her for being such a stubborn girl, but the minister said that after she grew up she would fall in line. She went to the local school and did well. Upon graduation, she attended a teachers' institute, but she never became a teacher. After her marriage to Hirss, she took courses in accounting so that she could take charge of the financial part of her husband's business and release his full energies to meet the more pressing problems of his fledgling firm.[11] She turned out to be his closest and most effective collaborator in all his entrepreneurial activity.

The major difference between *Rigas Audums* and other Latvian textile firms was that Hirss succeeded by innovating as rapidly as possible, whereas other firms—operating comfortably behind the protection of high import duties and, during the depression years, import quotas—felt no need for innovation and continued their traditional textile operations. And if one branch, such as the cotton industry, encountered any stiff domestic competition, the largest firms set up cartels or entered into protective "gentlemen's agreements."

Hirss, on the other hand, a veritable prototype of Joseph A. Schumpeter's entrepreneur, introduced all of his innovative methods and added others that Schumpeter had never listed.[12] Intuitively, Hirss seemed to know that "entrepreneurship is the ability to see unexploited opportunities."[13]

In the Latvian textile industry the usual raw materials were flax fibre, wool, and cotton. The flax was produced in Latvia; some of the wool was imported and some produced domestically; but all of the cotton came from abroad. From this starting point, Hirss pioneered in seven principal areas of innovation in the operations of *Rigas Audums:*

1. From the beginning *Rigas Audums* tried to find *new and more useful raw materials* for the production of items in wide demand. The first commodity produced by the firm was batting, a material almost everyone used as a lining in overcoats. At that time, it was customary to produce batting from coarse, cheap Australian wool, mixed with processed wool. An overcoat lined with this kind of batting often developed an annoyingly thick hem, as the result of the tendency of the processed wool to drop off the batting and the shoddy to settle in the hem. Furthermore, the wool inside the batting often cut through the lining like horsehair and became irritating to the wearer of the overcoat. Hirss's batting, by contrast, was made from high-quality Australian wool that was light and warm and did not disintegrate.[14] Although it was quite expensive, it proved its value.

2. Almost from the outset *Rigas Audums* introduced new

commodities. The manufacture of silk and rayon fabrics was
new to Latvia, because these textiles had formerly been available only when imported from abroad. Because new fabrics
were subject to the whims of changing fashion, new patterns
had to be introduced every season. To stay ahead of the volatile
fashion demand and the need for ever-changing patterns, *Rigas
Audums* established working contacts with factories in Paris,
Milan, Switzerland, and Germany, where the new seasonal de-
signs were created. Once *Rigas Audums* learned what was in the
offing for the next season, the firm selected patterns best suited
to Latvian climatic conditions. They redesigned foreign fashions
to make them more attractive to the Latvian public and more
suitable to the taste of the potential buyers. By the time the
latest foreign styles arrived in other Latvian shops, usually
Rigas Audums had already been selling them!

Hirss's firm stayed a few steps ahead of its competitors by
refining marketing requirements. A specially organized department of about twenty people working under the direction of
artist-designers turned out roughly eight hundred patterns each
year.[15]

3. The firm also attempted to introduce *new technological
changes in the production of existing commodities.* Since practically all of the textile machinery was foreign-made, either
German or Swiss, most Latvian firms had accepted it as designed and delivered. But, from the very beginning of his entrepreneurial activity, Hirss asked his foreign manufacturers to
meet his specifications and to undertake certain alterations in
machine design in order to make the machinery more efficient.
These improvements benefited not only *Rigas Audums* but all
other buyers of the equipment as well.

With the onset of the worldwide depression, introduction of
foreign exchange controls in Latvia in the fall of 1931 drastically
scaled down imports and made foreign-imported machinery very
hard to come by. From then on, foreign exchange was in the
hands of the bureaucrats, and private businessmen never knew
when their requests for foreign exchange allocations would be
turned down, or for what reason.

Because of this gnawing uncertainty, *Rigas Audums* set up

its own machine shop and began producing the necessary equipment for its own plant. To produce the most suitable textile equipment, Hirss and his technical staff would study and evaluate all the advantages of a particular piece of German-, French-, or Swiss-made textile machinery. Once they knew its most efficient components, they would combine and assemble them, adding their own refinements, to produce a new machine that uniquely satisfied their needs.

Structural steel and gears were ordered from local firms, but the other parts were made and assembled in the machine shop of *Rigas Audums*. Only the necessary electrical motors were imported. In this way, *Rigas Audums* acquired highly efficient textile machinery at roughly one-third the cost of a similar import.[16]

As another example of technological improvement, when an old boiler was found to be inefficient, alternatives were explored. The Ministry of Transportation's offer of old locomotives for possible use as boilers was turned down. After experts and cost analysts had made a careful study of the plant's needs, *Rigas Audums* set up its own power station with specially designed, powerful English-made Babcock & Wilcox boilers and German-AEG steam turbines for the production of electricity. Because the turbine exhaust was emitted under a pressure of five atmospheres, it could be used as a source of heat for the plant's dyeing section. This kind of technological adaptation led to a considerable saving on foreign-imported coal. *Rigas Audums* had to pay for the steam and electricity-generating equipment in three years, at a rate of 3,000 lats a month ($600.00). But, even including this extra expenditure in production cost, the total expense was still one-third less than it had been previously because of the higher efficiency.[17]

4. The firm also strove to *improve the handling of materials*. Once *Rigas Audums* started large-scale production of silk and rayon fabrics, it became apparent that these items could not be dyed with the same equipment and chemicals as other textiles. Machinery and equipment had to be specially adapted; new dyeing methods and dyes were needed in order to raise quality and cut costs. This time-consuming adaptation and change took

place over several years, but the challenges were successfully met.[18]

5. As to the *Taylorization of the work process,* the mechanization of the plant had progressed so far that it did not pay to institute assembly lines. Machines already did most of the work, and the operators merely had to take care of the machines and regulate their speed. As the weaving process became more and more automated, one operator could handle more and more looms. At *Rīgas Audums* one operator handled eight, then ten, and ultimately twelve looms, and this number would have doubled had not World War II intervened, forcing the firm to cancel an order from the United States.[19]

Effective operations of textile machinery required not only manual dexterity on the part of the operators but also a degree of technical knowledge about the equipment. The operator also had to know the characteristics of the materials and of the finished products, as well as quality controls. The better an operator knew all this, the more he contributed to the work process of the plant.[20] But where could *Rīgas Audums* find such workers? The basic human resource existed in Riga, and the firm's management decided to set up a training program for its young workers. Mrs. Hirss played an important role in launching this comprehensive activity. The operations of the different machines required a certain natural aptitude on the part of the workers. To check the mechanical aptitude of the future operators, the employment office screened its applicants carefully and had them evaluated by Riga's Industrial Aptitude Testing Institute. For its part, the personnel office tried to learn as much as possible about the applicants' feelings toward the job, their sense of responsibility, and their honesty; they also set up a Trade School for training mechanics. Whereas skilled and experienced operators worked an eight-hour shift, the trainees worked only six hours a day, spending evenings attending trade school classes. In some special instances, such as when an entirely new procedure for textile production was set up for which skills were lacking, the company even sent mechanics or trade school students abroad for training. The training program as a whole, and the Trade School in particular, was a success; its graduates discharged their functions efficiently and, as a rule, were promoted rapidly.

6. *Rigas Audums* also strove *to open up new markets*. Whereas today new markets for a specific product are gained by means of advertising, in the 1920s and 1930s this process in Latvia was still in its infancy. The producer himself, or some of his trusted representatives, had to acquaint all the textile merchants, almost one by one, with the characteristics and advantages of a new or particular textile. Most of the merchants preferred to buy from familiar, established textile manufacturers and rarely added new items to their stocks. For them, the buying and selling of cloth was a purely mechanical activity.

To persuade these conservative retailers to add *Rigas Audums* products to their line of fabrics was to open new markets. For example, *Rigas Audums* placed its batting in the stock of one of the largest textile retailers in Riga, but the batting remained virtually hidden on the store shelves and did not move because customers had no chance to see it. Hirss, who not only ran his plant but also sought outlets for his product, one day met with the owner of the department store, who preferred the batting made by competitors. To demonstrate the quality of his batting, Hirss placed a piece of paper on the counter, then took some batting made by a competitor and shook it. Soon the paper was covered with a thick layer of short shoddy. Next he shook a piece of his own firm's batting, and the paper remained clean. This demonstration was sufficiently impressive to gain an extra market for the Hirss product. Thereafter, this large textile merchant retailed only batting made by *Rigas Audums*. With each such successful personal demonstration, the firm enlarged its markets. Yet such basic successes were achieved by the innovative ingenuity of Hirss himself.[21]

7. Even *setting up new forms of business organization* was not alien to the management of *Rigas Audums*. During the first few years of Latvia's independence its textile industry remained disorganized, especially in its pricing policy. Some of the textile producers were in the habit of flooding the market with their fabrics, paying no attention to the market's ability to absorb this output. At the end of the season, unsold miles of textiles were

usually unloaded at greatly reduced prices, a practice that led
to substantial variations and fluctuations for the same fabric in
different stores. To cope with the uncertainty of never knowing
whether they would be compelled to reduce prices at the end
of the season, merchants usually added an extra percentage to
their selling price as a sort of insurance, in case price reductions became inevitable.

Despite this, *Rīgas Audums* managed to achieve price stabil-
ity for its products. First, all its fabrics bore the imprint "Rīgas
Audums," to prevent other fabrics from being sold under its
name. Then *Rīgas Audums* convinced its retailers to sell at
stable gross profits; that is, by uniformly adding 25-30 percent
to their purchase price. Those merchants who did not like suggestions and could not be persuaded to follow them were usually
deprived of deliveries for a while. And, if nothing could be
done to bring the recalcitrants into line, the firm simply dropped
them as customers.

In contrast to other textile manufacturers, *Rīgas Audums*
paid close attention to market conditions and did considerable
market research. Of course, in later years, with a payroll of
thousands of workers, the company had a special staff to carry
out marketing and market research. For instance, estimates were
made regularly of the potential demand for a particular fabric
so as to avoid market saturation. Thus, its fabrics did not go
to unsold inventories, nor did they remain sitting on merchants'
shelves; there was no need to resort to the old practice of un-
loading goods at almost any price. Consumers could rest assured that throughout the country its fabrics were sold at stable
prices.[22]

These traditional innovations, so clearly defined by Schumpeter, gave Roberts Hirss enough elbow room to demonstrate
his entrepreneurial prowess by expanding the dimensions of his
enterprise. But he was to go much further.

NOTES

1. B. F. Hoselitz, "Entrepreneurship and Traditional Elites,"
Explorations in Entrepreneurial History, Second Series, vol. 1,

No. 1, 1963, p. 36. The need to stress social surroundings in entrepreneurial action is vividly demonstrated by one of the pioneers in entrepreneurial research, Professor Arthur H. Cole, in his *Business Enterprise in Its Social Settings* (Cambridge, Mass.: Harvard University Press, 1965), pp. 65-79 and pp. 123-162.

2. Aizsilnieks, p. 265 and p. 295.

3. R. Hiršs, *Rīgas Audums* (Stockholm: Daugava, 1965), p. 30.

4. *Ibid.*, p. 35.

5. *Ibid.*, p. 37.

6. *Ibid.*

7. *Ibid.*

8. *Ibid.*

9. He died in 1972 in Florida.

10. *Ibid.*, pp. 20-21.

11. *Ibid.*, p. 24.

12. J. A. Schumpeter, *Business Cycles: A Theoretical, Historical, and Statistical Analysis of the Capitalist Process*, vol. 1 (New York: McGraw-Hill, 1939), p. 87. A full discussion of three important types of entrepeneurial activity is found in chapter 10.

13. I. M. Kirzner, *Competition and Entrepreneurship* (Chicago: The Uneversity of Chicago Press, 1973), p. 127.

14. R. Hiršs, *op. cit.*, p. 32.

15. *Ibid.*, p. 86.

16. *Ibid.*, p. 54.

17. *Ibid.*, pp. 57-60.

18. *Ibid.*, p. 36.

19. *Ibid.*, p. 111.

20. *Ibid.*, p. 63.

21. *Ibid.*, pp. 32-33.

22. *Ibid.*, pp. 86-89.

IX

The Midas Touch of the Innovator

In addition to the seven types of innovation examined in the preceding chapter, *Rīgas Audums* conceived, developed and applied others as well. Roberts Hirss's almost obsessive single-mindedness produced a Midas touch that brooked no obstacles.

During the firm's first years, lack of working capital was its most vexing problem. Hirss remedied this by his innovative ways of obtaining working capital from his foreign suppliers of machinery and raw materials and from the domestic buyers of *Rīgas Audums*'s new commodities.

Hirss had returned from Russia in 1920 without a penny. Nor could he save much from his relatively low earnings prior to the establishment of the company. He did not marry into big money, although the father of Mrs. Hirss lent him 1,500 lats (roughly $300) by mortgaging his farm.

Once in business Hirss asked, on a few occasions, for a line of credit at the Latvian Bank but was turned down, either because the bankers did not know him personally or perhaps because Hirss did not succeed in establishing proper banking contacts. Since Latvia was experiencing considerable tightness in the money markets in the 1920s, long-term credits were very hard to obtain. Under these circumstances, many newly established Latvian firms got credit by the dubious means of what were called "friendship" bills-of-exchange, the English counterpart being "accommodation bills."[1]

Commercial banks at times accepted bills-of-exchange for discount and advanced funds for from 90 to 180 days. When the bill fell due, instead of making the payment, the parties replaced the old bill-of-exchange with a new one, under the same signatures. Such short-term funds were often used to finance long-term investment and improvements. During the

depression years, when commercial banks called in a good number of short-term loans, or refused to extend them, many firms
felt the money pinch and had to close down. Since *Rigas
Audums* never played this credit game, it was saved from great
and unpleasant difficulties later on.

In the beginning, the firm's paydays were particularly harassing. To be able to pay wages due, Hirss had to run from
one retailer to another and virtually beg them to pay their
bills. He usually collected enough in this fashion and so never
missed paying his employees on time. Reminiscing about those
early days, Hirss later recounted the following episode:

> I remember our first Christmas in business, when after paying
> all wages and bonuses my cashbox was completely empty. Not a
> penny was left for the family. To get some money for the holi-
> days, we pawned for the duration of the Yuletide, my wife's
> violin, which she liked to play whenever she could.[2]

To augment the working capital of the firm, Hirss took in
two partners in 1926, but by 1932 he was again the sole owner
of *Rigas Audums.*

Roberts Hirss, a man from the countryside, was one of the
homines novi of capitalism who became successful innovators
in the industrial era. Ordinarily the working capital for such
men was provided by commercial banks; but Hirss was not so
lucky. More than once the Latvian Bank refused the credit he
needed. But, being a resourceful person, he found a substitute
source of credit in foreign suppliers of textile machinery and
raw materials. Also, his wartime experience in the giant Russian
textile mills and his personal references were useful in the postwar period in arranging finances. For instance, Swiss and German machine manufacturers supplied equipment on condition
that the bill for it had to be settled two years after installation.
During this interval, a substantial portion of the sum owed
for the new machinery would already have been earned.

For the raw materials, usually imported from Belgium or
England, the bill had to be paid within six months of delivery.[3]
If everything went well, delivered raw materials could be
worked up into salable output within two weeks. In that way,

credit extended by the raw material supplier provided extra interest-free funds prior to the payment of the bill.

Moreover, during the first two years after *Rigas Audums* had moved to its Kurmanova Street plant, its second location, it began production of men's knitted rayon scarves, which were in very brisk demand at that time. To assure themselves of a continuous supply of these scarves, a number of merchants made substantial payments in advance, thus providing the fledgling company with even more interest-free funds.

A second type of innovation that Schumpeter did not mention was *public relations, or public welfare concern for the labor force. Rigas Audums* promoted quality work and high output per worker through its wage system. As a rule, increases in an operator's output, properly recorded and verified, resulted in an automatic increase in wages. During the Great Depression years, when numerous textile producers lowered wages to compensate for depressed textile prices, *Rigas Audums* retained its established rates. Because workers appreciated this policy, productivity per worker rose considerably. By streamlining the production process, by modernizing equipment, and by better plant layout, production costs were cut; moreover, *Rigas Audums* apparently had no difficulty in selling its output. It prospered even in the depression!

Latvian industry suffered from strikes in some years, resulting in a staggering number of lost man-hours. The principal cause was the workers' dissatisfaction with the prevailing wage scales. But, not surprisingly, *Rigas Audums* did not have a single strike,[4] although the firm was one of the largest industrial employers in independent Latvia. But that is not all. From the 1930s on, its management paid a great deal of attention to its labor force. It considered a loom operator as part of the labor force, and the machine and its operator as complementary factors of production.

Keeping a machine in good operating condition is one thing, but keeping factory hands productive requires more than simply paying their wages. Hirss's company strove to help its work force solve problems of daily living. It tried to awaken and satisfy cultural needs, and it even attempted to develop some social life among its employees. Despite the paternalistic sound of all this, the firm's outlays for these social activities should not be viewed as utopian "'do-goodism." On the contrary, improving human relations among its hundreds of employees was not only rewarding for the work force but profitable for the firm as well. The rationale seemed to be: the more content the worker is, the less he worries about daily chores; the more tranquil his family life and the more enjoyable his nonworking hours, the greater the likelihood that he will work well. For these reasons, *Rīgas Audums* took what at the time was a rather unusual course in striving to improve human relations among its large labor force.

Latvian workers customarily went to work in old, worn-out clothing, often heavy, uncomfortable, and even dangerous for operating the machinery. To change this situation, *Rīgas Audums* designed and tested its own work clothes, with the hope that, once perfected, they could become mandatory for all employees. Similarly, the firm searched for a comfortable and safe type of work shoe. If everyone was provided with such shoes, it was thought, there would be fewer accidents and sick-calls.

To help cope with the problems of daily living, no matter how small, *Rīgas Audums* established, in 1936, a special *Mother's School*, the first of its kind in Latvia. Intended for the firm's women employees, the school provided instruction in the evenings. It's program consisted of such subjects as how to balance the household budget and how to maintain an inexpensive but healthy and nutritious diet for the family. It offered courses in infant nursing, first-aid, female hygiene, marital relations, and child psychology. In addition to home economics subjects, much attention was devoted to setting up an efficient apartment, with particular attention to cleanliness, using for demonstration purposes a two-room exhibit apartment with a kitchen that *Rīgas Audums* had built. Courses in psychology transmitted basic knowledge in human relations and offered guidance on how to avoid conflict in social intercourse and to appreciate and respect the opinions of other people. What today constitutes the basic core of Home Economics was actually presented some forty years ago by a private businessman to his own employees. Not many firms in America during the Depression Decade could point to anything comparable.

In addition to the Mother's School, *Rigas Audums* established a nursery for infant care. The firm had also made plans for a low-cost cafeteria, designed to improve the workers' nutrition, but this was not implemented because World War II intervened.

Cultural activities, seen as a means of improving relations with and among employees, brought about the establishment in 1934 of a choir. Its singers were devoted music lovers who practiced twice a week in the evening. Led by highly respected Latvian conductors, the choir gave frequent recitals. Also in the cultural sphere, the firm's employees had their own theater. Managed by an eminent Latvian stage director, it presented at least one play a year for the company's Christmas party. A special Christmas party for the children was also part of the Yuletide celebrations. As still another means of homogenizing the large body of *Rigas Audums* employees—to create a sense of community and give a sense of belonging—the company gave a number of well-attended parties each year for its employees.

Rigas Audums also initiated group outings designed to acquaint its employees with their native country. Employees were asked not to cut any wild flowers or bushes, to respect the national and natural monuments, and not to litter. Protection of the natural environment was thus being fostered some forty years ago by *Rigas Audums,* although other firms paid little or no attention to such matters on their outings. Their meticulous concern about littering tagged *Rigas Audums* employees with the nickname "The Lords."[5]

These concerns were all in the area of social welfare, or improved human relations, a clear demonstration of the idea that benevolent paternalism can be good business.

To recapitulate how far Roberts Hirss was ahead of his time: he stabilized and maintained an equitable wage system even in the midst of the Great Depression; he developed healthy and safe working clothes and footwear; he established a Mother's School that dealt with all the problems of daily living from first-aid to female hygiene; and, some forty years ago, he was already aware of the vital need for preserving environment.

This rapid growth did not mean that Hirss's entrepreneurial life was a bed of roses. Not at all. But he was the kind of man who believed that obstacles are there to be overcome. The Greeks have a saying that life is nothing but trouble, and Hirss welcomed all the trouble he could get. He could not live without it. He was a man of hot temper and his wife was often referred to as the "smiling lightening-rod" of *Rigas Audums*. As a steady person, she often and quickly restored Roberts' equanimity. But she was much more than his pacifier, so to speak. Hirss understood almost fifty years ago, when hardly anybody spoke of women's liberation, what a vital role a woman or a wife can play in business. He delegated numerous functions to his wife, discussed all major managerial decisions with her, and they launched all their innovations together. It is virtually impossible to say who decided what and where, for the two Hirsses decided things together. But, of course, in public only Roberts Hirss's voice was heard. His wife Alma remained a silent partner.

As his *Rigas Audums* grew and prospered, Hirss's main problem was not his competitors but the statist-oriented government of Ulmanis. The authoritarian Latvian government tried to establish in all vital branches of the economy at least one "national" enterprise, i.e., state-owned firm. *Rigas Audums* was too big to be overlooked in this endeavor. The squeeze on it started in a guise of innocence.

For instance, in 1937, the government created the *Vilnas Rūpnieks* (Wood Producer) corporation, which accounted for the major portion of the country's woolen industry. At the beginning of 1938, the Latvijas Kreditbanka bought out, after coming to terms on a voluntary basis—a forgotten euphemism from those years—the textile firm *Bufalo* and subsequently sold it to the government-owned *Latvijas Kokvilna* (Latvian Cotton) corporation. At the same time, the cabinet charged the Latvijas Kreditbanka with dissolving the cotton goods producers' syndicate, called the *Latvijas Kokvilnas Ražojumi* (Latvian Cotton Goods) corporation.

Of course, a similar fate was shortly in store for the rayon industry, and the major producer of rayon—*Rigas Audums*. The government's intentions could be seen from some incidents that Hirss experienced. At first glance these seemed unimportant, but they were particularly revealing upon further inspection. For instance, one day Hirss was invited to visit the finance minister, who generously offered him all the credits he needed. Hirss thanked the minister for his generosity but refused the offer. His intuition grasped at once that in such generosity might lay a trap. Had he taken the credits offered, it is conceivable that the government might have demanded the appointment of some political hack to the management board of the firm. If he had conceded, Hirss would have had to contend with a silent but extremely powerful partner not of his choice. To prevent such a possibility, Hirss rejected the credit offer without blinking an eye. His answer caused consternation among the bureaucrats, because it was previously unheard-of for any firm not to snap up such an offer. It was obvious that Hirss's firm had no liquidity problems; but, if that was the case, who were his financial backers? Everyone in Riga knew that Hirss had started his business venture in 1925 with almost empty pockets, and it was inconceivable that he needed no extra funds now.

Almost nobody, of course, really wanted to know, remember, or believe that for more than a decade Hirss and his wife Alma had worked for their firm with dedication and perseverance. Year after year they had ploughed back, selflessly, the firm's profits into their business. To the government officials, such charitable attitudes, bordering on calvinistic spartanism, was silly. The popular attitude in Latvia was that if you made money you should have a good life and live it up; after all, you can't take it with you. Hirss made lots of money, but he was not a social glamour boy, nor was his wife a society type.[6] In 1936, for instance, she granted an interview and revealed why the Hirss family lived the way it did:

> People with an active social life have very many social obligations. If one attends dinner parties, one has to reciprocate by inviting people to one's own home. My husband and I do not go

anywhere because we have neither the time nor the inclination. Perhaps our dedication to work is a bit one-sided, but our work in our entire life has been our aim, for which we have fought and struggled. . . . We never had even a beautiful apartment or expensive furniture. We did not even take the time to think about it. . . .[7]

Nor was Hirss bent on making capital of his importance. For instance, after having been decorated with the Three-Star Order, he was told that the president of Latvia wanted to see him and his wife, who was also so decorated, at an important social function of Latvian dignitaries. Hirss declined the invitation. He was his own man, apparently, and he took orders from no one, even a president.

The financial and social independence of the Hirss family was most perplexing, and people kept on asking and wondering: "Who finances Hirss? Are they foreigners? Maybe even Jews?" After all, the name Hirss, pronounced Hirshs, sounds Jewish. If so, then a large firm such as *Rīgas Audums* could not be permitted to remain in his hands, with all those sinister financial manipulators behind his back.

The thirties were years of extreme nationalism throughout Europe. For real or imagined reasons, in no time at all the government demanded the balance sheets and income statements of the firm and put a score of government accountants to work, scrutinizing every figure to uncover Hirss's financial "manipulators." But no such individuals or financial institutions were uncovered. The first assault by the corporative government of Ulmanis was successfully repulsed. The bureaucrats retreated and waited, licking their wounds.

In 1936 an event took place that created favorable preconditions for the next assault on the Hirss firm. The objective was to acquire the firm for transfer into state ownership. In 1931 England devalued the pound sterling and went off the gold standard. All the Scandinavian countries followed suit, but a number of countries decided to remain on the gold standard and retain the old exchange rate, almost at whatever costs.

France and Switzerland and, strangely enough, Latvia belonged to the so-called gold bloc. But in 1936 France decided

to devaluate its franc; on September 27 Switzerland followed,
and on the next day Latvia did the same. After the devaluation
of the lat, the pound sterling, which had been worth 15.58 lats,
was thereafter listed at 25.22 lats. This change in the exchange
rate meant that Latvian exports would be cheaper in England
and English goods more expensive in Latvia. For the Latvian
importers the price of the pound sterling rose by 62 percent.
After the devaluation, many firms that had large unsettled bills
stated in foreign currency found themselves in financial difficulties because now their obligations had increased enormously.

Foreign debts caused huge losses to many debtor firms. The
Ulmanis government exploited these difficulties for its own ends
and acquired numerous firms in trouble over obligations in
foreign currency. An example from the candy-making industry
will illustrate how it was done. A number of firms in this
industry had large, unsettled debts abroad for raw materials and
machinery. After the devaluation these firms could not pay the
swollen debts, and the *Latvijas Kreditbanka,* after "voluntarily
coming to terms," acquired the entire stock of two major candy-
making firms, the *Laima* and *Th. Riegert* corporations. The
latter was acquired for the explicit purpose of "liberating the
domestic market from the very strong influence of foreign capital in the industry." From these two firms was created one
"national" state-owned corporation, called *Laima.*

Hoping to find *Rīgas Audums* in similar difficulties after
devaluation, the Finance Ministry sent two of its certified
accountants to audit the financial situation of the firm once again.
Fortunately for *Rīgas Audums,* its foreign debts were not large
at that time. The firm had set up its own machinery and equipment shop, and its foreign indebtedness had gone down considerably before devaluation. The completed audit found the firm
in a solid financial position once again. So this round of the
sparring match also went to Hirss.

It is quite possible that *Rīgas Audums* was spared the
government takeover because of its unique legal structure. In
1934 *Rīgas Audums* was a publicly registered corporation of
which the Hirss family was the sole owner. The *Rīgas Audums*
corporation, however, owned only the machinery and equipment

—*not* the site or buildings; these were rented from Roberts Hirss, who was the legal owner of both. Consequently, if for whatever reason the government might acquire the firm, they could not acquire without great difficulty the site and buildings, without which the firm could not operate.

The last major assault against *Rīgas Audums* by the spreading corporativism was launched in the spring of 1939. Without warning, the government lowered substantially the import duty on silk fabrics and permitted them to enter Latvia in large quantities. It was expected that these huge quantities of cheap, foreign-made fabrics would compel *Rīgas Audums* to cut its prices and sell its fabrics at a loss. If the Hirss firm had to operate at a loss, the government would then have a convenient reason for taking over the firm in order to turn it into a "national" enterprise. To parry this cleverly conceived attack, Hirss went to the United States to purchase the most advanced weaving looms available to bring down his production costs even lower. As it turned out, the bureaucratic assault on *Rīgas Audums* did not have its intended punch. Although the price of the imported fabrics was low, its quality was lower. *Rīgas Audums* did not reduce its prices in the face of this contrived glut of rayon fabrics. It is true that the firm had difficulties in selling its spring assortment of fabrics, but whatever was left Latvians bought in the fall, when World War II began and the demand for cloth increased rapidly.

The firm managed to preserve its independence during the years of Ulmanis's rule, when the government restricted the activity of privately owned firms day by day, whereas the number of the so-called "national," state-owned or state-controlled enterprises increased rapidly. *Rīgas Audums* had won more than another round of the long, drawn-out boxing match: this time it actually was the end of the fight. Later on in his memoirs Roberts Hirss noted that the chairman of the Latvian Industrial Chamber and chairman of the Latvijas Kreditbanka, Andrejs Bērziņš, the chief advocate and driving force of the "national" enterprises, would have drowned him and *Rīgas Audums* in a ladle of gruel if only he could.[8]

Despite the continuous tug-of-war between *Rīgas Audums*

and the spreading government bureaucracy, the firm grew extremely fast. Its owner had ambitious plans for the future, but World War II intervened. Hirss's plans included the building of plants to produce cellulose and rayon fibers in order to eliminate the need for their importation.

Only three years after the establishment of *Rīgas Audums*, Hirss moved to neighboring Lithuania, where he set up a textile company, *Kauno Audiniai*, in 1928 in the city of Kaunas. The new firm bought machinery and raw materials on the same terms and from the same suppliers as *Rīgas Audums*, but some of its equipment came from the parent firm in Riga. Although the managerial and technical staff of *Kauno Audiniai* came from Riga, the training of Lithuanians for the various skills was started at once.

To overcome the language barrier, the Latvian arrivals from Riga studied courses in the Lithuanian language, and the Lithuanians learned Latvian. Since the two languages are closely related, remarkable progress was achieved quickly and language difficulties soon surmounted. By 1939 *Kauno Audiniai* had more than 2,500 employes on its payroll and was actually bigger than *Rīgas Audums*. The Lithuanian firm carried on social activities similar to those in Riga.

One of the unexpected windfalls of being a multinational company occurred when Latvia introduced extremely tight foreign exchange controls in 1931, and Lithuania held off until the fall of 1935.[9] Even though Latvian bankers were not too kindly disposed toward Hirss, and the bureaucrats who controlled foreign exchange were even less inclined to be accommodating to requests for German marks, dollars, and pounds sterling, with *Kauno Audiniai* in Lithuania, where foreign exchange was not controlled, Hirss had considerable elbowroom for financial maneuver. Latvian economic bureaucrats resented this double-back-up system because they could not stifle Hirss's entrepreneurial activity.

He had also planned to set up similar plants in Finland, Sweden, and Norway, and had studied both the market and the textile industry in those countries. In Norway, he had already bought a textile firm, *Miron-Aktieselskap*, which was awaiting machinery from Riga. But the outbreak of World War II destroyed all his plans. The textile business was Hirss's life; it was not just a means to the good living he could have enjoyed. Neither he nor his wife Alma craved luxury, high society, or political influence. For Hirss the entrepreneurial life was a relentless quest for change. One prominent Latvian journalist described Hirss as follows: "A man with a hot temper, volcanic energy, and a genius's capacity to work: he does not walk, he leaps. It is very difficult to say what guides him: the voice of reason or deep intuition."[10]

With the outbreak of World War II, Roberts Hirss's concern was not so much for his firm but for his life and his family. He had experienced the early Soviet totalitarianism on his own skin in a Russian prison, and he had known of the horrors of the Stalinist terror in the 1930s. He understood people and was alert to the big power politics of the time. Also, he was very much afraid for his small native country. He knew the wheels of fate were slowly grinding it into dust. So, in the late fall of 1939, he left Latvia and, together with his wife and three young sons, via Stockholm and Switzerland, came to the United States, where he started anew. He established the *Roberts Hirss Company* and prospered again in the textile business so familiar to him. But that is another story. His firm in Riga is now operated by the Soviet-Latvian government, and even today bears its old, honorable name of Rīgas Audums.[11] Tradition, it seems, cannot so easily be ground to dust.

NOTES

1. Such bills of exchange are drawn exclusively for the purpose of raising funds. An "accommodation bill" does not represent any real account between the accommodation parties but is drawn only in order to be discounted. If accommodation bills are abused by the parties' constantly drawing bills on each other, covering one bill with the proceeds of the next, such bills are called "kites" or "windmills." See A. Warren, *Some Business Terms and Concepts Explained* (Sweden: Hugo Gerbers Förlag,

1950), pp. 7-8; and Philip A. S. Taylor, *A New Dictionary of Economics* (London: Routledge & Kegan Paul, 1969), p. 173.

2. R. Hiršs, *op. cit.*, pp. 43-44.

3. *Ibid.*, pp. 45-46.

4. *Ibid.*, p. 68.

5. *Ibid.*, pp. 71-78.

6. For an interesting contrast see, for instance, J. Kārklinš, *Preses karalis*, New York, 1962, vignettes on the Latvian glamour girls of the time, pp. 45-50.

7. "Rīts," April 5, 1936, Latvian newspaper, published in Riga.

8. Hiršs, *op. cit.*, p. 109.

9. "Lithuanian Exchange Control," *The Economist*, vol. 121 (1935), p. 662.

10. J. Kārklins, *Latvijas preses karalis* (New York: Grāmatu draugs, 1962), pp. 154-155.

11. R. Deičs, *Rīgas Audums* (Rīga: Latvijas valsts izdevniecība, 1957), 111 pp.

X

Notes on Types of Entrepreneurial Activity

Incredible as it may sound, the entrepreneur is the neglected man in contemporary economics. Economists know and say that the entrepreneur is important in the economic evolution of nations, so "it is somewhat paradoxical that the entrepreneur has been ignored in much of the recent literature of economic history."[1] He has been neglected in economic theory as well. Even though the history of the Industrial Revolution reads like a roll call of inventors and successful innovators and the role of the entrepreneur is frequently mentioned in the works of classical economists, he remains "a shadowy entity without clearly defined form and function."[2]

The creative role of the entrepreneur was first popularized in the nineteenth century by the French economist Jean Baptiste Say, who, writing in the tradition of the English classical economists, argued that "entrepreneurs provide the connecting link between product and factor markets."[3] But it was not until the twentieth century that the most elaborate explanation of the nature and function of entrepreneurship emerged. The author was Joseph A. Schumpeter (1883-1950), the versatile Austrian-born economist, who taught at Harvard during the last twenty years of his life. His original work, published in German in 1911, became available in English only in 1934 as *The Theory of Economic Development*. However, during the Depression Decade and the three postwar decades academic economists paid little attention to entrepreneurship, although Harvard's Research Center in Entrepreneurial History did very useful work on it in the 1940s and 1950s. Today, only Professor Wilhelm Treue, who teaches in Göttingen and Hanover, West Germany,

117

devotes considerable attention to this topic, especially in the quarterly, *Tradition*, which he publishes. In fact, it is not too much to say that in the last four decades the role of entrepreneurship has virtually disappeared from the textbooks of microtheory.[4] In the late 1960s, Professor Harvey Leibenstein noted that "the received theory of competition gives the impression that there is no need for entrepreneurship."[5] In the contemporary world of microeconomists, who are exclusively concerned with the "allocation of scarce means among competing ends,"[6] assuming often perfect knowledge of the market, entrepreneurship becomes as unnecessary as a fifth wheel. But once the assumption of perfect knowledge is dropped, everything changes; at that moment, "it is this entrepreneurial element that is responsible for our understanding of human action as active, creative, and human rather than as passive, automatic, and mechanical."[7] In fact, at the end of 1973, Professor Israel M. Kirzner of New York University made a persuasive plea to his fellow economists for the readmission of entrepreneurship into the texts of microtheory.[8] His hope is that it will usher in a new era in which entrepreneurship will again become respectable in the eyes of academic economists. In the past, economists were "quick to emphasize the importance of entrepreneurship for economic development, [but] they [were] as a rule reluctant to get involved in its study."[9] The reasons for the prejudice of most intellectuals against the entrepreneur, apart from those just cited, are listed by Schumpeter as follows: (1) large masses of the people are poor, while the entrepreneurs represent a very small but very rich minority; (2) ignorance of the social function of entrepreneurship in relation to profits is widespread; and (3) the idea is common that production will take place even in the absence of the entrepreneur.[10]

A brief review of Schumpeter's theory of the unique role of innovators—how they generate profits and how they affect the ups and downs of the aggregate business activity—may provide a useful background for the layman in evaluating the performance of *Rīgas Audums*.

Schumpeter's exposition of his theory begins with an examination of a given stationary economy, in which the same repetitious and routinelike activities take place year after year and in which innovative entrepreneurs do not exist.[11] If more shoes are needed, more labor and more leather will be used, and shoes will be produced in the familiar, conventional manner. In a static economy of this type, net profits tend to be zero, because businessmen merely recover all their production costs, including a return for their own work. By contrast, in a dynamic economy, the need for more shoes would be met by new methods of producing shoes. These new ways constitute for Schumpeter a "creative response,"[12] which becomes the very essence of economic change. As one writer has put it, the "means of production which heretofore served certain static uses are diverted from this course and placed in the services of new purposes."[13] Schumpeter calls this process of diverting the existing means of production to *new uses* "the effectuation of new combinations," which he believes represents "a step outside the boundary of routine . . . and it involves a new element."[14] It is this new element of innovation that is the principal entrepreneurial function, a phenomenon of leadership in economic life.

Schumpeter gives three reasons why the entrepreneurial function is relatively rare and why it is difficult to achieve. First, if someone conceives of a new way to produce something new, he is out of customary channels, "which means the individual is without the data that normally influence the decisions of a manager. He must guess and depend more on intuition than on data."[15] A second difficulty lies within the businessman himself and his fixed habits of thinking. To break through the institutional preconceptions and prejudices of the market requires certain rare qualities—such as a certain personal force and vigor. Only a few have this unique combination to overcome the existing routines of the market place. Those who do, those few who break out of the economic rut, perform what Schumpeter calls the entrepreneurial function that is "of its own kind," or *sui generis*. Third, in order to introduce a new product on the market, the entrepreneur has to overcome the reaction and resistance of the buying public, which calls for a special kind of conduct.[16]

But what, according to Schumpeter, precisely constitutes

innovation? In a general way, he says, an innovation "is a setting
up of a new production function."[17] More specifically, innovations take the form of *producing new commodities, organizing
technological changes in the production of commodities already
in use, opening up new markets, discovering new sources* (of
raw materials), *standardizing work, improving the handling of
material,* and *setting up new management organizations.*[18] The
management aspects of innovation involve also the breaking of
an existing monopoly or the setting up of a new monopoly. By
carrying out all of these innovations, singly or in combination,
the entrepreneur earns more than just the customary return on
his business activities, and his extra profits represent the innovator's reward for doing new things. A notable assumption in
Schumpeter's theory is that his innovators in general have been
poor and therefore must borrow funds from the banks. Another
salient point is that Schumpeter's above-normal innovational
profits are not permanent. A swarm of imitators, fired by the
example of the innovator's high profits, begin to copy the innovation in hopes of sharing the bonanza. This process of imitation
reduces the erstwhile innovation to routine business practice,
and "the profit slips from the innovator's grasp," to use the
felicitous phrase of Schumpeter.[19] Thus, he points out, without
relentless innovation, private enterprise lacks the luster of continuous change, the dynamism that keeps it from becoming
routine.

Schumpeter was very much aware that with the evolution of
the capitalist system innovations gradually become more and
more mechanized and routinized. Indeed, he states, his innovative entrepreneur was more representative of the competitive
capitalism of the nineteenth century than of the present-day
"trustified" capitalism.[20] In the highest stages of big-corporation
capitalism, he asserts, innovation will originate in the corporate
research labs and drawing boards. At this stage the individual
innovator's profits cease to play the role they once did.

In the United States and Western Europe today innovation is
standard practice in all successful corporations. If they do not
innovate, they fail within a decade, as one recent study has
shown.[21] But, in addition, the individual innovator still prevails,

as the profiles in the business section of the Sunday *New York Times* would seem to indicate.

Schumpeter's analysis turns on entrepreneurial action, innovation, and the credit mechanism in a free market economy(without, for example, the mandatory ceilings on prices and wages of 1971-1974 in the USA). What is always overlooked, however, is that the innovations reviewed in Schumpeter's analytical framework produce *socially useful goods*. Therefore, the interaction between the innovator and the consuming public represents a community of interests. For example, when housewives want a good peeling knife, the innovator who can meet this demand stands to make a fortune. If, however, his particular knife is not successful, he stands to lose his shirt, so to speak. Not so under a direct controls situation or under a repressed inflation.

During the two world wars of this century, the United States, United Kingdom, Nazi Germany, and Fascist Italy suspended the operation of market forces, although nominally private and corporate ownership of the means of production remained intact. All belligerents established systems of priorities for the allocation of raw materials, machinery, and consumer goods. Wartime priority allocations served two basic purposes: they aided producers to obtain the necessary inputs from suppliers, and they enabled producers to plan and execute contracts in the order of wartime priorities. Ships, planes, tanks, guns, submarines, and ammunition represented top priority items, and the wartime allocation system was designed to subordinate civilian to military demands. Price, wage, and rent controls, rationing of consumer goods, and direct allocation of raw materials, manpower, and housing became the main pillars of the new economic structure, replacing the price mechanism that existed before the war. During a war, economic policy aims at maximum utilization of existing material and human resources in the struggle for victory. Winning the war becomes the primary social objective of the nation, with everything else subordinated to this goal, especially if the war is total and only unconditional surrender of the enemy will end it.

Given this paramount objective, the distribution of resources between public and private uses, or between guns and butter, can be brought about by a simple formula: in order for a warring nation to achieve maximum striking power, it must drastically cut the resources available to the consuming public while maintaining the indispensable minimum of food and consumer goods necessary for the health and incentive of the general public. The sustaining of high motivation for war depends upon the judicious division of available resources between the private and war-related sectors. In reviewing the wartime experience it becomes obvious that when government demand is urgent, credit is virtually unlimited, and there is no limit on government spending to obtain the necessary resources for war. With a fully employed economy, the aggregate demand exceeds aggregate supply at constant prices. This excess is known as the *inflationary gap,* and its control constitutes the very crux of wartime inflation. Direct controls, in the form of fixing ceilings on prices, wages, and rents, together with rationing and priority ratings,[22] are all designed to cut down the civilian propensity to consume and to release resources for a "hot war," like World War II, or an "investment war," such as has been carried on in the Soviet Union since 1929. These types of controls are a government's most powerful weapon for curtailing aggregate spending, assuring rough justice in the distribution of consumer goods, and maintaining social peace at home.

The existence of the entire gamut of physical controls in conditions of excess aggregate demand is called *repressed inflation.* [23] Under repressed inflation the monetary income anyone earns does not automatically entitle him to claim goods, since these can be purchased only if currency is accompanied by rationing coupons, rationing points, or special purchase permits. Monetary income, insofar as it can be spent on legal purchases and rations, retains stable purchasing power. However, those portions of money income that cannot be spent legally, because of a lack of rationing coupons, do not have legal purchasing power and must, therefore, be either saved or spent on the black market. Thus, under a system of repressed inflation, *two* kinds of monetary income exist side by side: income endowed with legal purchasing power, and income rendered useless for legal purchases.

This excess income may, of course, be used for paying taxes and fees or saved for the future.

The difference between income endowed with legal purchasing power and income without it constitutes *monetary overhang*, or *potential purchasing power*. The size of this potential purchasing power depends upon the degree of repressed inflation or the comprehensiveness of direct controls. The more universal the direct controls, the larger will be the amount of potential purchasing power and the greater will be the tendency for the marginal value of income above the legal expenditure level to fall to zero. On the other hand, if only a part of the economy is subject to physical controls, while the other part—that producing nonessentials—is free of controls, income earned above the legal rationing expenditures can be used for purchases of goods and services in the uncontrolled sector at going market prices. Of course, the greater the free uncontrolled market, the greater the importance of making money and the greater the incentive to work.[24]

However, any system of physical controls, whether it be designed to release resources for "hot" wars, or to finance "investment wars" (as in the Soviet Union or mainland China), or "to keep the cost of living down" (as in Israel from 1949 to 1952), or to implement "industrial disarmament" (as did the Allies in the occupied zone of Western Germany from 1945 to 1948), causes the emergence of what the present authors choose to call a *perverse*, or *negative, entrepreneur*.[25] He utilizes the existing institutional and legal framework of controls to introduce innovations that enable him to make substantial profits, regardless of the low utility of his product. Since all prices are fixed, usually on the cost-plus basis, what the entrepreneur in such circumstances does is to design a *new* commodity, one not produced before the price-fixing because of its virtual uselessness.

Since full employment prevails and most essential goods are subject to rationing, the potential purchasing power usually produces ready money burning the lining of everybody's pockets. Or, it often spills over into the black market when people feel impelled to buy anything they can. In such spend-happy milieus, the perverse, or negative, innovator makes his appearance, producing luxury or semiluxury items generally considered useless or marginally useful in peacetime, when market forces impose some economic discipline on market participants. An example of this occurs when prices of all necessary goods have been frozen and business establishments find that they can make more money by producing "new" items. They therefore submit the design for such "new" goods—accompanied by cost estimates, supported by the statements of production engineers—to the price-fixing authorities. If approved, the "new" goods usually get a higher price simply because costs of designing the "new" goods have been demonstrated to be high. It thus becomes lucrative to produce nonessentials and to suspend the production of such typical essentials as forks, pots, knives, dinnerware, electrical switches, and drinking glasses.

To illustrate: After the defeat of the Third Reich, the Allied occupying powers retained the entire gamut of physical controls in that country for the purposes of bringing about Germany's economic and military disarmament.[26] Since virtually all prices remained frozen at 1936 levels and production was low because of destruction, reparations removals, and the lack of raw materials, costs of production were so high that most firms were losing money. One way out of this loss squeeze was the production of "new" commodities. Since prices were generally fixed on the cost-plus basis, high production costs per unit or design outlays on a "new" commodity sufficed to obtain profitable prices from the Allied price-fixing authorities. In the postwar period there was a veritable flood of "new" commodities. Some 5,000 price increases were granted for so-called new goods[27]—including ashtrays, fancy lamps, dolls, chandeliers, glasses of the oddest shapes imaginable, all kinds of wall and ceiling decorations, and other *low-utility items*—while the production of badly needed forks, pails, pots, and other *high-utility* products essential for daily living was stopped.

Similar developments took place in Israel. For instance, one manufacturer stopped producing drinking glasses, which had to be sold at a low fixed price, and turned to the production of fancy liqueur glasses, which could be marketed at profitable prices.[28] As a result of this reorientation of production, the development of many branches of consumer goods was retarded. A similar development took place in Israeli agriculture. Since potatoes and vegetables had to be sold at low fixed prices, most of the kibbutzim turned to the cultivation of flowers, which were free of price controls. It simply paid to raise flowers, regardless of whether people had vegetables or not. As another example, bread, which was price-fixed but not rationed, was used by Israelis as a "substitute fodder" for raising chickens, ducks, and rabbits, instead of for human consumption. In Israel, in 1951-52, the legal price of one kilogram of chicken was four times that of bread, and the black market price was twelve times greater.[29] Since sufficient quantities of feed grains were not available, kibbutzniks and other individuals fed their animals the cheap bread and sold the animal proteins so generated on a free market at very lucrative prices.

In sum, under conditions of repressed inflation, the "negative," or "perverse," entrepreneur exploits the legal and institutional factors to make profits. The fact that he produces "junk" goods does not bother him. His concern is to make money, not to worry about the usefulness or uselessness of his output. In such a manner, factors of production are rerouted into the channels profitable to these unique trailblazers, or so-called innovators. In postwar Germany, for instance, conditions were such that "the self-interest of individuals and of firms was strictly opposed to the common interest."[30] According to another source, the incentive to produce was in almost "directly inverse proportion to the social utility of the product."[31] The more useless "new" product proposed to the price-fixing authorities, the greater the probability that it had not been produced before the price freeze began, and the easier it was to obtain a profitable price, since people bought anything that was offered for sale. As a result, Western zones of occupied Germany prior to the currency reform of 1948 had what the late Professor Wilhelm Röpke facetiously called a "hair oil—ash tray—herb tea economy."[32]

The end of World War II marked the beginning of the end

of the Western colonial empires and the subsequent emergence of new sovereign states. Britain abandoned its colonial empire without violence at home and without any serious economic consequences.[33] The French, the Dutch, and the Belgians followed suit reluctantly. Only Portugal (until recently) and the Soviet Union still hold on to their colonies. This process of decolonization and the emergence of newly independent nations —both salient features of the contemporary world—have placed emphasis on three major trends that are confronting economists, political scientists, and historians. The first is the rise of the idea of economic change and the concurrent disappearance of contentment and fatalism, a novel concept that began to take hold of men's minds in the eighteenth century. The second is the resurgence of nationalism in the new nations. The third is the conviction that the scientific spirit of rational analysis will supplant the traditional forms of society, the faith that technology will raise the material and social standards of all developing countries.[34]

Despite the lofty ideas that the new countries have about their future, two-thirds of the world's people live in poverty. The economic analysis of these poor but sovereign countries demonstrates a recurrent pattern of lack of *material infrastructure*—in the form of adequate roads, ports, canals, sewers, irrigation systems, and silos, and inadequate *human infrastructure* for raising the levels of material well-being rapidly—that is, in terms of sanitation, health facilities, public hygiene, nutrition and functional literacy. In addition, the existing *institutional infrastructure* (the local customs, social mores, administrative apparatus, police courts, bureaucracy, social fragmentation, corruption, and the lack of vertical mobility) is inimical to material progress. It is geared instead to the preservation of a static, nonindustrial, and technologically backward society. And static human and institutional infrastructures, in turn, result in a dearth of local entrepreneurial talent.[35] This lack of entrepreneurial talent constitutes "a hindrance to economic development under free-market economies in most of the economically underdeveloped parts of the world."[36]

The entrepreneur is a *rara avis* in the emerging nations,[37] which raises the interesting question of why young men do not become entrepreneurs. Are they afraid of uncertainty? Or has the government to a great extent taken over the entrepreneurial functions? If so, is Schumpeter's theory of economic development applicable to present-day developing countries? The answer to the last question is generally *no,* because Schumpeter's innovator has today been generally replaced by the public "business leader" of the large modern corporation or government agencies.[38] In the developing countries the private sector is usually very weak, and industrial development is fostered by government bureaucrats.[39] Moreover, popular pressures compel governments to raise the living standards of the masses rapidly and to push the investment activity into social overhead capital (or infrastructure), something that the private sector usually does not do. The existing social milieu is consumption-oriented, which, of course, means that aggregate savings remain low. And lastly, because most of the technological innovations are imported from the industrially advanced countries, one scholar argues that Schumpeter's theory of development is virtually irrelevant for underdeveloped countries.[40]

Another writer has pointed out that since the governments of developing countries invest heavily in the infrastructures, the private entrepreneurs may find that they can get the best manpower available only at competitive prices, for they would have to bid up wage rates to lure labor away from the public sector.[41] Thus, in countries where the governments appear to be out to crush the private sector, Schumpeterian production-oriented entrepreneurs do not appear.[42] The government becomes the entrepreneur.

Other economists have also noted that Schumpeter's innovator theory is largely inapplicable to underdeveloped countries because governments play the role of entrepreneurs.[43] Whereas Schumpeter's theory of development was derived from experience in capitalist countries and his emphasis was on production, today's underdeveloped countries are demand-oriented. As these governments strive to raise the living standards of the masses, they take over the economic leadership that in the capitalist era of the nineteenth century was left to the private entrepreneur.[44] Still another scholar has argued that Schumpeter's theory is obsolete and is not adequate for the analysis of economic growth in either the developed or developing countries. It takes more than the transplantation of the latest technology from the industrially advanced countries to achieve successful modernization and/or industrialization, and what seems to be needed is an economic innovation in the Schumpeter-ian sense.[45]

But if Schumpeter's innovator is not applicable to underdeveloped countries, where does that leave us? Is it really true that with the predominance of government in economic life innovators have disappeared? What is the nature of governmental control over the private sector?

One of the most comprehensive discussions of this complex problem recently has been provided by Professor Gunnar Myrdal, in his *Asian Drama, The Challenge of World Poverty* and *Against the Stream.*[46] As a rule, Myrdal maintains, development plans are cast in terms of public investment, whether in social overhead or in extractive or manufacturing industries. To implement these plans, governments use *positive* and *negative* operational controls. The *positive controls*, Myrdal continues, are designed to stimulate, facilitate, and induce investment and consumption by providing technical assistance, subsidies, tax holidays, credits on easy terms, low prices on products, services from the public sectors, low cost foreign exchange, and tariff protection against foreign competition. The *negative operational controls* are designed to limit production, consumption, and investment in whatever sectors may be decided on by bureaucracy. These negative controls are generally implemented by harassing and bullying private entrepreneurs, by restricting investment activity in certain fields, by imposing excise duties, by denying foreign exchange, by rationing, and by raising cost components.[47]

In the nineteenth century, Myrdal reasons, the Western countries achieved economic modernization through foreign trade, which enabled them to become industrialized through an "export-led" pattern. Today's underdeveloped countries cannot follow suit, however, by reasons of *low elasticity of importing* in the industrialized countries, substitution of synthetic

products for the raw materials traditionally supplied, lower raw
material import requirements because of technological innovation, the tariff restrictions in Western Europe and America, and
lastly, their exploding populations that eat up, so to speak, some
of their exportable raw materials.[48] The result is an ever-
widening foreign trade gap, which is reflected in an acute
shortage of dollars, pounds sterling, Swiss francs, and deutsche
marks. Moreover, the widespread use of positive and negative
discretionary controls, in contrast to nondiscretionary controls,
leads to corruption. Since the mistrust of capitalism and private
business is pervasive, and the Marxist tradition deeply ingrained
in bureaucrats and intellectuals,[49] the only way someone from
the private sector can get things done is to offer bribes. Myrdal
reports that in Southeast Asia businessmen have to bribe
high officials and politicians in order to put through a business
deal and have to bribe officials high and low in order to run
their business without too many obstacles.[50]

The prevalence of acute foreign exchange shortages and
the existence of tight foreign exchange control give rise to what
the authors chose to call *the red-tape-cutting innovator.*

Since underdeveloped countries exist in a twilight zone between feudalism and capitalism—with fragmented markets for
goods and services, where economic behavior is not governed by
rational calculation of costs and profits—bribes are indispensable
for closing the existing gaps. On the basis of the widespread
bribe-taking, structural change is slowed down. However, this
very system of pervasive discretionary controls has enabled a
particular type of entrepreneur to emerge, one who knows how
to evade, avoid, and exploit these controls and make money by
doing it. Such an entrepreneur is a far cry from Schumpeter's
production-oriented innovator. He is also different from the
"perverse" entrepreneur producing "junk" goods in conditions
of repressed inflation. The entrepreneur operating in underdeveloped countries is not production-oriented at all. In fact,
he makes money by producing, for the most part, nothing. His
forte is slipping "speed money" to corrupt officials. He sells his
services to businessmen of the private sector. Since this entrepreneur usually finds a way to cut "a path through the jungle

of administrative controls,"[51] what his entrepreneurship really
amounts to is to cut the red tape of government regulations. In
India, for example, it is reported that a foreign exchange license
on the black market fetches "anything between 100 percent
to 500 percent of its face-value" if sold.[52] Clearly, then, in underdeveloped countries the red-tape-cutting entrepreneur can make
substantial profits from knowing his way through the administrative maze of discretionary controls. Since virtually all developing countries practice discretionary controls, including tight
foreign exchange controls, they encourage the emergence of
nonproducing entrepreneurs, who thrive in the hothouse atmosphere at the expense of the Schumpeterian production-
oriented innovator.

The preceding notes on entrepreneurship are in no way
intended as an exhaustive survey of the subject. They are merely
an attempt to single out the three types of entrepreneurial activity obtaining in the twentieth century. They are useful as a
yardstick for measuring the part played by one privately owned
firm, *Rigas Audums,* in a statist-oriented institutional milieu.
They may also point a way for emerging nations to foster structural change by giving greater scope to the private sector.

NOTES

1. J. H. Soltow, "The Entrepreneur in Economic History,"
The American Economic Review, vol. 58, no. 2, (May, 1968),
p. 84.

2. W. J. Baumol, "Entrepreneurship in Economic Theory,"
The American Economic Review, vol. 58, no. 2 (May, 1968),
p. 64.

3. E. Roll, *A History of Economic Thought,* 3rd Ed., Engle-
wood Cliffs, N.J.: Prentice-Hall, 1956), p. 321.

4. I. M. Kirzner, *Competition and Entrepreneurship* (Chicago: The University of Chicago Press, 1973), pp. 8, 20, 31-32,
69, 75.

5. H. Leibenstein, "Entrepreneurship and Development,"
The American Economic Review, vol. 58, no. 2 (May, 1968),
p. 72.

6. Kirzner, *op. cit.*, p. 32.

7. *Ibid.*, p. 35.

8. *Ibid.*, p. 75.

9. A. P. Alexander, "The Supply of Industrial Entrepreneurship," *Explorations in Entrepreneurial History*, Second Series, vol. 4, no. 2 (1967), p. 136.

10. J. A. Schumpeter, "Der Unternehmer in der Volkswirtschaft, von heute," in *Strukturwandlungen der Deutschen Volkswirtschaft*, vol. 1, 2d ed., edited by B. Harms (Berlin: R. Hobbing Verlag, 1929), p. 305.

11. J. A. Schumpeter, "Unternehmer," *Handwörterbuch der Staatswissenschaften*, vol. 8 (Jena: G. Fischer Verlag, 1928), p. 481.

12. J. A. Schumpeter, "The Creative Response in Economic History," *The Journal of Economic History*, vol. 7, no. 2 (1947), p. 150.

13. E. Schneider, "Schumpeter's Early German Work, 1906-17," *Review of Economics and Statistics*, vol. 33 (1951), p. 107.

14. J. A. Schumpeter, *The Theory of Economic Development*, translated from the German by Redvers Opie (Cambridge, Mass.: Harvard University Press, 1934), p. 84.

15. *Ibid.*, p. 85.

16. *Ibid.*, p. 87.

17. J. A. Schumpeter, *Business Cycles: A Theoretical, Historical, and Statistical Analysis of the Capitalist Process*, vol. 1 (New York: McGraw-Hill, 1939), p. 87.

18. *Ibid.*, p. 84.

19. Schumpeter, *The Theory of Economic Development*, p. 153.

20. J. A. Schumpeter, *Capitalism, Socialism and Democracy* (New York: Harper and Bros., 1942), p. 132.

21. The Staff of the Wall Street Journal, *The Innovators* (Princeton, N.J.: Dow Jones Books, 1968). In the contemporary chemical industry, for instance, permanent evolution is the order of the day, with more than 500 new chemicals every year; see C. Levinson, *Capital, Inflation and the Multinationals* (London: G. Allen & Unwin, 1971), pp. 168-192.

22. C. Pigou, *The Political Economy of War* (New York:

Macmillan Co., 1941), pp. 137-150. This is only one arbitrary choice among many studies on the subject.

23. W. Röpke, "Offene und zurückgestaute Inflation," *Kyklos,* vol. 1 (1947), pp. 57-71. An early but excellent analysis among many.

24. H. K. Charlesworth, *The Economics of Repressed Inflation* (London: G. Allen & Unwin, 1956), pp. 35-48.

25. N. Balabkins, *Germany Under Direct Controls: Economic Aspects of Industrial Disarmament, 1945-1948* (New Brunswick, N.J.: Rutgers University Press, 1964), p. 162.

26. *Ibid.,* pp. 44-80.

27. U.S. Office of Military Government, Manpower Division, "Unemployment and Underemployment in the Bizonal Area of Germany (mimeographed), 1949, p. 18.

28. A. Rubner, *The Economy of Israel: A Critical Account of the First Ten Years* (New York: F. A. Praeger, 1960), p. 65. See also N. Balabkins, *West German Reparations to Israel* (New Brunswick, N.J.: Rutgers University Press, 1971), pp. 96-118.

29. *Ibid.,* pp. 13, 59, 267.

30. F. A. Lutz, "The German Currency Reform and the Revival of the German Economy," in *Economica,* vol. 16 (1949), p. 122.

31. International Chamber of Commerce, *The Economic Conditions of Germany Today and Its International Repercussions* (Paris, 1947), p. 33.

32. W. Röpke, "Das Deutsche Wirtschaftsexperiment: Beispiel und Lehre," in *Vollbeschäftigung, Inflation und Planwirtschaft,* edited by A. Hunold (Zürich: E. Rentsch Verlag, 1953), p. 271.

33. J. Strachey, *The End of Empire* (London: V. Gollancz, 1959), p. 214.

34. W. Hochwald, "An Economist's Image of History," *Southern Economic Journal,* vol. 35, no. 1 (1968), pp. 3-16.

35. E. E. Hagen, *On the Theory of Social Change* (Homewood, Illinois: The Dorsey Press, 1962), pp. 175-180.

36. L. E. Davis, J. R. T. Hughes, and D. M. McDonald, *American Economic Histroy,* 3d ed. (Homewood, Illinois: R. D. Irwin, 1969), p. 104.

37. T. C. Cochran, "Entrepreneurship," in *International Encyclopedia of the Social Sciences*, vol. 5 (1968), p. 90.

38. B. F. Hoselitz, "The Entrepreneurial Element in Economic Development," in *The Challenge of Development, Theory and Practice*, edited by R. J. Ward (Chicago: Aldine Publishing Co., 1967), p. 122.

39. W. Malenbaum, "Government, Entrepreneurship, and Economic Growth in Poor Lands," in *World Politics*, vol. 19, no. 1 (1966), pp. 52-68.

40. H. C. Wallich, "Some Notes Towards A Theory of Derived Development," in *The Economics of Underdevelopment*, edited by A. N. Agarwala and S. P. Singh (New York: Oxford University Press, 1963), p. 201.

41. P. S. Laumas, "Schumpeter's Theory of Economic Development and Underdeveloped Countries," *The Quarterly Journal of Economics*, vol. 76 (1962), p. 655.

42. *Ibid.*, p. 657.

43. H. W. Singer, "Obstacles to Economic Development," *Social Research*, vol. 10 (1953), pp. 19-20.

44. D. Rimmer, "Schumpeter and the Underdeveloped Countries," *Quarterly Journal of Economics*, vol. 75 (1961), p. 429.

45. V. W. Ruttan, "On Schumpeter and Development," *The Philippine Economic Journal*, vol. 4, no. 1 (1965), p. 57.

46. G. Myrdal, *Asian Drama: An Inquiry into the Poverty of Nations* (New York: Twentieth Century Fund, 1968); *The Challenge of World Poverty: A World Anti-Poverty Program in Outline* (New York: Pantheon Books, 1970); and *Against the Stream: Critical Essays on Economics* (New York: Pantheon Books, 1973). See also N. Balabkins, "Myrdal versus the 'Armchair Economists': His Asian Drama," in *Il Politico*, vol. 37, no. 3 (1972), pp. 509-524.

47. Myrdal, *Asian Drama*, p. 903.

48. *Ibid.*, pp. 1160, 919, 946, and 669.

49. Myrdal, *Against the Stream*, p. 78.

50. Myrdal, *op. cit.*, pp. 937-958.

51. Myrdal, *Asian Drama*, p. 928.

52. *Ibid.*, p. 924, n. 1.

Postscript:
A Recapitulation of the Latvian Example of Entrepreneurship and Government Bureaucracy in Conflict: Some Lessons for Developing Countries

After the end of World War I, Latvia began its independence with a paralyzed infrastructure. Its *material infrastructure* was virtually gone; roads were in ill-repair and virtually unpassable, ports were both mined and silted, without cranes, docks or warehouses. The railroads were denuded of their rolling stock, and the telephone and telegraph network was a nightmare of malfunction. Latvia's *human infrastructure* was particularly hard hit by the long years of bloodletting. The flower of Latvian manhood had been mowed down, gassed or crippled in World War I. The *institutional infrastructure* was in shambles, wrecked by the various military occupation authorities and the bloody revolution, which promised material success on this side of the grave to all toilers and called for the complete elimination of all vestiges of the "bourgeois" social order. Whatever was left was hardly useful to the new sovereign state of Latvia. Radical changes, adaptations, and innovative adjustments were necessary to make the new, small country viable, but all these adjustments in the institutional infrastructure could hardly be achieved overnight.

With the infrastructure debilitated to this degree, Latvia's birth was painful. The state of ill-repair of the infrastructure affected unfavorably the country's agriculture and industry. But that was not all. The so-called *directly productive activities,* agriculture and industry, were undergoing drastic structural changes as well. Since almost one-half of the entire territory of Latvia consisted of large estates, owned mostly by the German-speaking Baltic nobility, the country's agriculture called for immediate reforms so as to give land to the landless Latvian peasants. The landless peasants got their land, but the erection of farm buildings, acquisition of cattle and horses, tools, implements, seeds and other farm gear called for a huge outlay of capital funds, which the war-ravaged Latvia did not have.

The revival of industry was equally difficult on account of drastic structural changes. Before the war, Latvia's large-scale industry had produced primarily for the vast Russian markets. But after gaining independence the new Soviet state sealed its borders, and Latvian industry had to become suppliers primarily of the domestic market. Foreign markets were eventually found, especially for butter, timber, and plywood. The industrial firms, the majority of which were in the hands of non-Latvians (primarily German), were operated to a great extent with foreign capital. In a number of industrial branches, these firms had set up powerful cartels and syndicates. Their modes of operations were not beneficial for the Latvian masses, and their attitude toward Latvian-owned firms was hostile. For reasons too numerous to elucidate, the ruling political and administrative circles of independent Latvia in the 1920s and 1930s did everything in their power to increase the number of government-owned enterprises and state monopolies. This effort seemed to be primarily the result of the bureaucracy's need to acquire a bigger voice in the economic affairs of the country. These trends became even more pronounced after May 15, 1934, when a coup d'etat transformed the country from a parliamentary democracy into a one-man dictatorship.

Under the circumstances it was difficult, and at times hardly possible, for privately owned domestic industrial enterprises to emerge and be successfully operated by the country's native sons. Yet, despite the prevailing anti-free-enterprise milieu, such firms did exist, and some of them even prospered.

The story of *Rigas Audums* demonstrates that private enterprise could grow and develop when an owner-manager was not routine-oriented, but was rather a creative, daring, and innovating entrepreneur. Roberts Hirss found new raw materials, developed new production methods, built new machinery, introduced new commodities, discovered new markets, obtained new sources of funds for expansion, and paid considerable attention to human relations—all innovative steps taken well in advance of his contemporaries. The result was the successful and continuous growth of his firm and the opening up of a number of well-paid jobs.

Roberts Hirss's entrepreneurial conflicts with Latvian bureaucracy were legion, but through his innovative methods he was able to surmount them. In the 1920s he did not get any credits from the Latvijas Banka and later on he did not ask for any. Starting with 1931, when the Latvian government introduced tight foreign exchange controls, he ran a continuous battle with foreign exchange controllers. After May 1934, when Latvia became a dictatorship and the Ulmanis government was setting up "national" enterprises in almost all industries of Latvia, Hirss was constantly challenged by the spreading bureaucracy. The Finance Ministry offered him generous credits, but he turned them down for fear of having a government-appointed political hack added to the management board of his firm. Having done so, the question arose, "Who finances Hirss—international Jewry?" In the extremely nationalistic decade of the 1930s, questions of this type led to the government's demand for the firm's balance sheets and income statements in order to uncover his supposed financial backers and manipulators. But no such individuals or institutions were ever found. And he kept on prospering, despite the country's trend toward a proliferation of government bureaucracy, until his successful escape from Latvia in the late fall of 1939.

What lessons might the developing countries of the 1970s learn from Latvia's experience of *entrepreneurship and government bureaucracy in conflict,* as demonstrated by the example of *Rigas Audums* during the 1920s and 1930s? Despite the billions of dollars in grants and loans that have gone to the world's developing countries since the end of World War II from the "have" countries in Western Europe and the United States, the developing countries have remained poor. Government and bureaucracy are *the* agents of public investment in these countries (bureaucracy has been growing by leaps and bounds), and yet their capacity to raise the living standards of the mass of people has been a failure. The majority of African and Asian intellectuals and bureaucrats of the 1960s and and 1970s, who were educated in the liberal tradition in England and America during the interwar period and after World War II, brought home anti-free-enterprise biases, not to mention Marxist leanings. Very much like the Latvian bureaucrats and intellectuals trained in prewar Tsarist Russia, where the government acted as an entrepreneur, most contemporary African and Asian ruling circles appear to be suspicious of, if not downright hostile to, the private sector. As a result, free and private enterprise has been relegated to a modern "Cinderella," marginal role in the structural-change process of the developing countries. Of course, inhibiting cultural factors—such as the practice of expanded families, tribalism, and the absence of a "protestant work ethic"— and the control of numerous sectors of the economy by European expatriates, or Syrian, Lebanese, Greek, or Indian business communities, have made it difficult for the native entrepreneur to assert his rightful role in the economy of his country after it has gained political independence. However, the fact that almost all postcolonial governments in Africa and Asia have acted as if they knew better, had more resources at their disposal, and could do everything faster and on a larger scale than private entrepreneurs has been, in our view, one of the principal obstacles blocking their modernization efforts, as it was in the case of Latvia. This is the *explicit value premise* of this volume.

Given this value premise, may we ask some pertinent and impertinent questions? To date, the unilateral transfer of funds from the world's rich countries to the recipient governments in Africa and Asia has not been crowned with success in raising the material well-being of the masses of these people. The most glaring example of imbalance has been the recent instance of India's pursuit of nuclear power while 200 million of her population are idle and suffering from malnutrition, disease, and abject poverty. Is it not, perhaps, time for the Western donor countries to try an alternative approach to the structural-change problems in the developing countries? For instance, what would *happen* if the Western donors inspired recipient governments to raise and develop cadres of native entrepreneurs and unshackle the private sectors of the economy from the interference of bureaucrats, who seem to care chiefly about their own comfortable city lives?

Since the past methods of administering aid funds have been failures, isn't it time to give the necessary incentive, protection of earnings, and a better deal for the private and native entrepreneur? A change in economic policy of this nature might usher in an Era of Native Entrepreneurship, which could put Mercedes-driving bureaucrats into Volkswagens and Fiats. Such a radical departure from the past policies could conceivably unleash forces that, like the Industrial Revolution of eighteenth- and nineteenth-century England, might propel the economies of the developing countries away from the dead-center of the "backwardness trap" and toward a viable future. What of Adam Smith's eloquent plea two centuries ago to replace the petty mercantilist restrictions and state interferences with the activities of private entrepreneurs and merchants? Didn't England transform its economy, as if by magic, after the mercantilist creed was abolished? This reminder of the policy change two hundred years ago in England may amuse those modern economists who believe that the answers do not lie in history. It may also be ridiculed by self-seeking bureaucrats in the developing countries. Nevertheless, if this suggestion serves to make those bureaucrats a bit uneasy—as they ponder that this kind of policy change could get serious consideration and could even be tried and implemented—it will have fulfilled our hope.

Index